IT'S ONLY MANSLAUGHTER

It's Only Manslaughter

Steven M Silverberg

Copyright © 2024 by Steven M Silverberg
All rights reserved. No part of this book may be reproduced in any manner whatsoever without written permission except in the case of brief quotations embodied in critical articles and reviews.
First Printing, 2025

Dedication

DEDICATED TO THE PEOPLE WHO MADE ME
WHAT I AM TODAY
RACHEL, MARA, ELI AND MAYA

FORWARD

IT'S ONLY MANSLAUGHTER -

A Fictionalized Account of the Real Life Experiences of a New York City Prosecutor

Over the decades there have been many new laws and court decisions interpreting and applying the laws that have altered the way criminal investigations and prosecutions are conducted. As a result of those changes and changes in our society in general, some of the police and district attorney's procedures described in this book would be inappropriate, or possibly illegal today and therefore have changed. While the book is based upon actual events, the details have been fictionalized and, in many instances, they are presented because they are examples of the more bizarre circumstances I encountered and/or are only events that could have occurred roughly fifty years ago, in the context of different laws, societal norms and during a huge upsurge in crime in New York City.

At the time of the events described there were approximately four hundred homicides in a single year, just in Brooklyn, one of the five boroughs (counties) making up New York City. In contrast, in 2023 a total of 386 homicides were reported in all of New York City's five boroughs. Due to the frequency of the violence and the stress placed on those of us who were forced to deal with it, my early experience with law enforcement was often strange and, generally, unlikely to be repeated today.

Over the years I have shared several of these stories with people I know. Many of them urged me to write a book about these incidents because they are so beyond anything we regularly read about or see depicted on television or the movies. I hope you will agree with their request that I turn these stories into a book.

INTRODUCTION

In the early 1970s I unexpectedly started my legal career as an assistant district attorney in the Brooklyn, New York District Attorney's Office (Kings County DA). It was a time of such significantly high levels of crime as to make the statistics in New York City today look mild. Due to the nature of the office, the overwhelming amount of criminal activity and the societal customs of the time, my experiences as a prosecutor were often bizarre, grim and occasionally funny.

This book is a fictionalized account of my experiences becoming an assistant DA and working as an assistant DA. The events on which this book are based are true. They are also often tragic. To avoid raising old fears or emotions among those who may have been connected directly or indirectly with any of these events and may still be alive, more than fifty years later, I have changed some of the details of these situations from what actually occurred. I have also altered names, dates, locations and in some cases the age, gender and/or ethnicity of those involved. In addition, due to the volume of criminal activity in New York City at the time, there were many similar incidents on a nearly weekly basis. Therefore, in reading this book, if a description leads you to believe we are talking about you or someone you know, more than likely that is not the case. Nothing in this book is presented for the purpose of upsetting or embarrassing anyone. Rather it is presented to demonstrate the unusual experiences I had a long time ago that, for the most part, cannot be repeated today and in some instances may even appear made up because they are so strange.

Steven M. Silverberg

1

CHAPTER 1
A TWENTY-FOUR-HOUR SHIFT

It was a Tuesday at 2 a.m., I was riding in the backseat of a police patrol car speeding along the Brooklyn Queens Expressway heading into one of the most violence prone neighborhoods in Brooklyn. There was a light drizzle which just added to the depressing aspects of what I was about to do. At that moment, I had very little information about what had occurred at our destination. All I knew was someone had been shot and killed. I, for reasons I will explain, was on my way to the scene of the homicide.

As we sped along during what was to be my last night "riding homicide" I began to think about why I found myself in the back of a patrol car at two in the morning. Here I was, a young lawyer, a little less than two years out of law school heading to the location of the third murder I had to be involved in investigating in less than twenty-four hours.

My job title was Assistant D.A. in the Brooklyn District Attorney's Office. After a little more than a year in the office, I had been assigned to the Homicide Investigations Bureau. Supposedly, it was a "prime" position in the office but, at two in the morning in the back of a police car with rain spattering the windows, it didn't feel like a particularly prime position to be in.

Part of my job was going to the scenes of homicides, taking statements from any witnesses the police had located and meeting with the police to work with them in commencing the investigation into the homicide. This meant working with the specialized squad of detectives assigned to homicide investigations. The police detective homicide groups, or districts, each covered several police precincts in each of the five boroughs of New York City. Due to the frequency of criminal incidents in the different neighborhoods throughout the borough, some homicide districts, like the district we were heading towards, were much more active than other homicide districts.

As the patrol car exited the highway it made a few turns and pulled up in front of a group of older-attached row houses, visible through the haze created by a combination of the rain and the glow of streetlamps. I got out of the patrol car. As soon as I closed the car door, the patrol car made a sharp U turn with tires squealing and immediately took off.

The police officers who had dropped me off had done their job of delivering me from my relatively nice, relatively safe neighborhood to the scene of a killing. Now in a neighborhood I, and apparently the two officers from my neighborhood, would generally avoid, even in daylight, I suppose even armed police officers wanted to get out of there as quickly as possible. Hence, the screeching tires as they were obviously rushing to get back to the relative safety of my neighborhood, which was their regular area of patrol.

Near one of the lampposts there were two police officers standing on the sidewalk. As I began to approach them to ask for the detective in charge, another patrolman, who looked to be about twenty-five and in good physical condition, came running down the steps leading from one of the row houses behind us. Based upon the speed of his exit from the house, my initial impression was that there was some sort of emergency. He paused briefly when he reached the curb, glancing furtively at us. Then, without saying a word, he bent over the curb and started vomiting into the roadway. Clearly that was his emergency.

Usually, the police were stoic at the locations of the various homicides I had been unfortunate enough to see in my nearly nine months going to the scenes of homicides. They often acted as if all the blood and gore was just part of a day's work. I had never seen a policeman react in this way at the scene of a homicide. In fact, on more than one occasion I observed police officers eating their lunch or having coffee while they guarded the scene that still had a dead body or bodies present. This officer's reaction gave me a true sense of foreboding about what I was about to see in the house he had just rapidly exited.

Typically, one of the male court stenographers who was assigned to the DA's office, would meet us at either the scene of the homicides or, in cases where the body had been removed, the stenographer would meet us at a police station. This was in case we had to take any statements from witnesses or if there was a suspect we wanted to question. In that way we could have a certified transcript of any statements taken which could be used later as evidence, if necessary.

Frank, the stenographer assigned that night, showed up just as the patrolman was losing his dinner into the street. Frank took one look at the patrolman and announced, "I am not going in there. If we have to take statements, we can do it somewhere else. You are not doing to me what you did to Pat this afternoon."

Even though it was now past 2 a.m., I was approaching the end of my typical twenty-four-hour, 6 a.m. to 6 a.m., rotation as an assistant district attorney in the Homicide Bureau. At about 2 p.m., in the afternoon of the day before (but still part of my current twenty-four-hour shift), I had been called to the scene of a double murder in a bar. The location of the afternoon murders was in a neighborhood that had levels of violence like the neighborhood we were now in.

The scene from the previous afternoon that Frank was referencing took place in a small, dark, and dreary bar room. The room consisted of a small bar that looked like it would seat about eight people, and the only table was the pool table that was near the entrance door. To compound things, it was a rather gruesome scene with two dead bodies. The two bodies were sprawled, face down on the floor, just inside the doorway of the bar, taking up nearly the entire space between the pool table and the entrance. They had clearly been shot in the back of the head, execution style, with the floor around them covered in blood, pieces of skull and bits of brain tissue. To add to the unpleasantness, the bodies had apparently been there for a couple of days and the odor of decaying flesh, somewhat like spoiled cheese, permeated the air. The status of the bodies raised additional issues as to why they had been there for so long and why no one had noticed the two dead bodies until they were reported that afternoon.

One witness was present at the scene. He was standing outside with the detectives. Usually, we would have taken the witness to the police station for questioning. However, the detectives were still working on checking out the scene of the crime and the surrounding neighborhood to see if they could get any additional information, as well as waiting for someone from the medical examiner's office to make a preliminary evaluation of the two corpses.

The police were hopeful they might locate someone else who had seen or heard something. Unfortunately, the one witness they had located could only provide some basic information about the bar hours and other operational issues unrelated to the specific crime.

After a brief discussion with the detective in charge, it was agreed we should take the witness' statement as soon as possible, as getting whatever information we could, no matter how minimal, might aid the investigation. Based upon the circumstances, the only practical location to take the witness' statement at that time was in a small, equally bleak room at the back of the bar.

Unfortunately, the only way to reach the room in the back of the bar where we wanted to take the statement of the witness was to step over one of the bodies sprawled on the floor nearly blocking the entrance to the barroom. This would cause us to unfortunately receive the full visual impact of the gore splattered on the floor, as well as the full effects of the aroma of decaying flesh in the room.

Pat, the stenographer assigned to assist me earlier that afternoon, agreed with the arrangement for taking the statement in the room at the back of the bar. We started to enter the bar when Pat saw the patrolman, who was guarding the bodies. As if the disgusting scene in front of us was not enough to make someone sick to their stomach, there was the patrolman, sitting at the bar, eating a large, overstuffed egg salad sandwich. The sandwich was so large the patrolman had to hold it in both hands. To say the least, it struck me as odd that the patrolman was eating his lunch at the scene of a gory double homicide, with the strong odor of rotting flesh all around him.

However, the sight of the brains on the floor and then the egg salad sandwich in the patrolman's hands struck Pat right in the gut. Pat took one look at the bodies and the patrolman, turned, and he ran outside. Just as the patrolman Frank and I were observing about twelve hours later, Pat deposited his last meal in the gutter before returning to the bar to take the statement of the witness.

From Frank's statement to me it was clear that Pat had obviously complained about having to look at decomposing bodies (or perhaps the egg salad in the same room as decomposing bodies) to Frank. Thus, the clear explanation for Frank's statement about not doing the same thing to him that I had done to Pat.

Frank's protest over entering the scene of the current homicide, before he had any evidence of what he was about to see, other than the patrolman leaning over the curb and depositing his last meal was clearly enough evidence for Frank that what was going on inside the row house was more than he wanted to see. Since I did not yet know what was going on in the house, I responded to Frank as best I could:

"Look if there are any witnesses we are going to have to take their statements. But I promise I will do whatever I can to keep you from having to view whatever is going on in there."

Standing there on my last night "riding homicide," watching a patrolman vomiting into the street, while listening to Frank complain about having to go inside to the scene of a homicide that had not yet been described to us but, where there was obviously something quite unpleasant, I thought about how I now found myself doing this crazy job of going to the scene of a homicide, as an attorney.

2

CHAPTER 2
HOW DID I GET HERE?

After working two summers in a law office during college, I had decided to become a lawyer. I started out with specific goals, none of which involved being at the scene of a homicide, standing in the rain in a poor, violence prone neighborhood at 2 a.m. I attended a law school that had been rated one of the top ten in the country. I had grades that were good enough to put me in the top quarter of my class. In most circumstances that would have been sufficient to get a job at a respected large New York law firm. During my last semester in law school, I applied for jobs at some of the top law firms in New York City.

Unfortunately, as I learned then, timing is everything. A serious recession got in the way of my career plans. No one was hiring, or if the larger firms were hiring, they were hiring one new attorney instead of the ten they had the year before. I was not only invited to interview at some of the top law firms in New York, I was called back for second and even third interviews at some of the firms. Yet, each time someone else was the single new hire for the year. As the days and weeks drifted by, I became increasingly concerned about finding a job as an attorney somewhere.

One day there was a job posted at the law school placement office for a position with the Brooklyn District Attorney's Office. It was not what I had been looking for, but it was already two months past graduation from law school and there were not a lot of prospects for new law school graduates that year.

Recently married, I needed a job. In fact, there weren't any other prospects. Why not apply to the District Attorney's Office, nothing else was available. It was 1971, the job paid $12,500 once I passed the bar exam and was admitted to practice. The top law firms were only paying $15,000 starting salary in those days. The DA was not offering a top salary, but for a newly married twenty-five-year-old, in1971, it was not a bad salary, especially in view of the fact that there did not appear to be any alternatives.

I submitted a resume to the District Attorney's Office and not long afterwards, was notified to come to the office for an interview. I put on my best twenty-five-dollar gray suit that had two pairs of pants to choose from and went for an interview, having no idea what to expect. Upon arrival I was ushered into the office of the Chief Assistant D.A., who rose from behind his large ornate desk to shake my hand. He was a man of average height in his fifties who looked fit for his age, with dark hair, wearing a dark brown suit, white shirt and dark blue tie.

After a firm handshake, he sat me down in front of his massive dark wooden desk. As I sat in a low chair about two feet in front of the desk, he sat on the front edge of the desk directly opposite and looming over me. After a short introduction, he proceeded to pose hypothetical situations, asking how I would handle each possible situation for which he provided details, while probing me as to what crimes I thought may have been committed in each situation. The hypotheticals were quite specific, ranging from the theft of cars to robberies and assaults. He pressed me, seeking my level of knowledge of various criminal laws that might apply to each situation. Then he would press me on the applicable procedures and how, if I was hired, I might approach prosecution of the various criminal acts and defenses described to me.

His position looming over me was clearly intended to intimidate me or at least to see if he could intimidate me. Each time I answered the Chief Assistant's questions, no matter what I said, he took the opposite position. If he described a fight and I said one of the parties could claim self-defense, he would challenge me stating there was no evidence in the hypothetical that he was assaulted first. He would then press me for an explanation of the position I had taken. He and I went back and forth with, "why that position, but what about this position?"

After pummeling me with questions about a particular hypothetical for several minutes, just as I would begin to feel comfortable with the back and forth on that issue he would move on to the next hypothetical situation. Then he would repeat the process of cross examining me as to my opinions, until he moved on again to another hypothetical crime and criminal.

He grilled me on multiple aspects of criminal law, multiple criminal activities, and multiple issues a prosecutor might face. I had one major problem. The only criminal law I had any experience with was a required criminal law course I had taken during my first semester of law school, nearly three years earlier. After taking the course, I concluded I did not need to study any more criminal law. I had no interest in practicing criminal law.

Instead, I intended to seek employment at a large New York City law firm and pursue a career in corporate law. To fulfill my naive concept of a proper legal career, I took courses in subjects like mergers and acquisitions, corporate taxation, accounting for lawyers, securities law, the Uniform Commercial Code and civil, rather than criminal procedure law. Criminal law was the furthest thing from my mind.

Throughout law school I continued pursuing my dream of a career in corporate law until the recession got in my way. Why would I need to study more criminal law than the one course required for graduation? After all I was headed for a career as the attorney for corporate titans in a large "Wall Street" law firm, with no criminal law practice.

To bolster my corporate credentials, I worked part time at a large New York City real estate company during my last year of school. One of the executives even offered to get me an interview at the large law firm that serviced the real estate company and other large corporations. But in my interactions with the lawyers in the law firm that served my employer, I found them to be rude and condescending. I felt that if they treated me with such disrespect when I was calling on behalf of a client, that being a new young employee at the firm would be even more unpleasant than my experiences with them as the representative of a large multi-million-dollar client.

So, there I was now, unexpectedly applying for a job as an assistant district attorney, seeking to practice criminal law in one of the busiest prosecutor's offices in the country. The Chief Assistant, of a nearly two hundred fifty lawyer office, was grilling me on the finer aspects of criminal law and procedures.

Being young, needing a job and, now four months after turning down the offer to be introduced to the large firm that serviced the real estate company I worked for, I tried my best to push back at the challenges posed by the Chief Assistant who was grilling me. My primary thought, as we went back and forth, was that he probably did not want to hire someone who could be easily intimidated.

As luck would have it, the one thing that I really needed for this interview was something I had already learned well during college and then law school. Before even going to law school, I had worked for two summers for an attorney who was in solo practice. As he had a lot of litigation and often had to appear in more than one court in a day, he often sent me to answer court calendars involving various motions. I questioned how I, as a college student, could appear in court on his behalf. He told me to "just announce to the judge that you are a clerk in the office, not an attorney, and ask permission to address the court."

I don't know if it was because I was tall and therefore people often thought I was older, but as a result, my nineteen year old self, having just finished my freshman year of college, actually was allowed by various judges to argue motions in the New York State Supreme Court in Manhattan, Brooklyn and the Bronx and other courts in New York City.

I never understood why I was allowed to do that, but I always made it clear I was not an attorney before participating. Perhaps things were less strict in those days, or judges were more easygoing? Those strange circumstances gave me some interesting experiences, as a teenage college student, arguing the pros and cons of various legal issues before judges in many of the courts in New York City.

My most memorable Court appearance, before entering my sophomore year of college, was a motion before a judge in Manhattan Civil Court. I again advised I was not a lawyer. After the other lawyer and I presented our respective positions. the judge ruled in my client's favor. As we walked into the hallway, the furious opposing attorney, apparently upset about losing the motion to a teenager, grabbed me by the collar, pushed me against the wall and said "tell your boss to stop screwing around." He then walked away quickly before anyone witnessed what he had done.

In addition to the unusual fact that I had actual court experience, in those days, every law school class was very much just like this interview. A barrage of hypotheticals, followed by challenges to every statement you made.

A professor would call on you and ask you to explain some judicial decision that had been assigned for review. He (in those days rarely a female professor) would then proceed to tear apart your analysis. Whatever you said would be challenged. Any position taken by a student would result in a demand by the professor for an explanation of the position. If you were not one of the approximately one third of students who dropped out during the first year of law school, you learned to stand your ground against the onslaught of verbal challenges, be logical in your responses and argue your position as best you could.

The law professors could be brutal and nasty if you folded under their barrage of questions. On one occasion a professor was cross- examining a student who was doing a poor job of responding. We were in a large lecture hall and the professor, a tall thin man in his sixties, was on a slightly raised platform. After finishing with the student, the professor reached into his briefcase, took out a small glass bottle and stepped off the platform. As he walked down the aisle between rows of seats, he approached the student he had just torn to pieces verbally. The professor then reached out with the bottle in his hand. In a loud voice, to be certain everyone in the lecture hall could hear what he was saying, he said: "here, take this. It is a bottle of formaldehyde. You need it since you are dead anyway."

He handed the glass bottle to the student, turned on his heels and went back to his lecture. Nothing further was said as the rest of us snickered. This sort of abuse was a regular part of many classes. Even with those professors who were not downright nasty, class participation was a constant intellectual and verbal challenge.

Therefore, after experiences like those I endured in law school, being politely, but firmly grilled by the Chief Assistant DA, was not a new experience. Following the law school process, I went back and forth with the Chief Assistant arguing every point. Even though I had little idea of what I was talking about. I tried to be as logical as possible. He continued to sit on the front edge of his desk looming over me. He continued asking me one question after the other, and arguing with every point I made, in a continuing attempt at intimidating me.

Finally, after about forty-five minutes, we finished. He went around to the back of his desk and sat down. He quietly made some notes. I waited breathlessly assuming he was about to tell me it was nice meeting me and I would hear from them, meaning "you blew it." After he finished making his notes in a notebook on his desk he looked up at me.

"Steve, the District Attorney makes the final decisions on hiring but I am going to recommend you. You will have to come into the office again next Tuesday to meet with the DA and be interviewed by him. I have one piece of advice for you before you meet with him."

"What is the advice?"

Leaning slightly forward, he looked over his glasses. "Study some criminal law, you, don't know any."

Clearly my law school training at spunk outweighed my total lack of knowledge of criminal law. In an office of almost two hundred and fifty prosecutors, apparently having the ability to stand up and logically argue your position was a trait they valued over knowledge of the statutes. I suppose he also hoped I would learn the statutes before I got into anything too complicated. In fact, I learned later that the office did provide some training.

The following week I had an interview with the District Attorney. I had studied some criminal law during the preceding week and was prepared for another session of cross examination. However, he apparently left that bit of fun to the Chief Assistant. The District Attorney, a short gentleman who also appeared to be in his fifties, sat at one end of a very large conference table. I sat in the middle. He asked me a few questions about my attitude toward certain legal issues relating to criminal prosecutions. There were no hypotheticals or challenges to my responses. Then, after about ten minutes of rather pleasant conversation, he told me I was hired.

Two weeks later I reported for work, as a newly minted "Criminal Law Investigator" the title the office gave recent law school graduates who had not yet been admitted to the Bar as attorneys. It was September, in those days the July bar examination results would not be announced until December. Once the results were released it took up to several months to complete the paperwork and the swearing in as an attorney. Therefore, I had to await admission as an attorney before I could formally become an assistant D.A.

However, working for the District Attorney law graduates were permitted to undertake many of the law related activities involved in prosecutions before being sworn in as attorneys. Therefore, I was able to work in different departments of the office before I was formally admitted to law practice.

Yet, as I was to learn, like most everything else in the office, the personnel practices of the office were a little strange. Even though I was hired and was already beginning work that Monday, when I arrived for my first day of work, I was asked to fill out paperwork that included providing the name of a reference. The instructions indicated the person providing the reference could be a relative, so long as it was someone I did not live with. As I was already a bit of a wise guy (a trait I developed more fully over time), I gave them my mother's name and address and identified her as my mother, thinking they would never contact her, or tell me to provide a different name. To my amazement they wrote a letter to my mother asking her for a reference.

A couple of weeks later my mother called to tell me she had received a letter from the Brooklyn District Attorney's Office seeking a reference for me. I asked what she did. "I responded right away and told them how very proud of you I am."

Back in 1971, employee screening processes were less stringent for prosecutors than they often are now for cashiers in a supermarket. In fact, about twenty years after I left the office, I learned that someone I had worked with, and who had continued as an assistant D.A. for those next twenty years, was discovered to have never been admitted to the practice of law. I guess they never asked his mother if he had passed the bar exam.

3

CHAPTER 3
CRIMINAL COURT

During my first few months in the office, as a Criminal Law Investigator, like the other newly minted employees of the office, I spent my time following assistant DAs around in different departments. The purpose of these exercises was for us to learn the procedures and pick up knowledge of criminal law that we lacked. Clearly, I had already demonstrated I knew nothing about criminal law and procedures when I was interviewed.

Finally, in early December I was informed I had passed the bar examination that had been administered in July. Due to the high volume of crime and the need for more prosecutors, there was a somewhat expedited process to complete admission to practice law for people who worked for district attorneys' offices in New York. As a result, I was admitted to practice law a couple of months before some of my law school friends who had gone into other areas of law practice. The one and only advantage to working for a DA.

Like every other experience I had those first years, the bar admission process was somewhat unusual. For example, we had to provide information on every place we had lived since birth and the source of the information we provided. It was never clear to me why where I lived at age one would somehow impact my ability to practice law.

Since I had no idea of the address of the apartment where we lived when I was four years old, I went to my usual source for confirmation, my mother and listed her as my source. We had to also list any run in with the law, including traffic tickets. Therefore, I dutifully listed the ticket I received when I was eighteen for running a stop sign.

The last step before being sworn in by a judge was an interview with a member of the "character committee." This was an attorney who was to check you out to be certain you properly completed all your paperwork and had no criminal nor other nefarious background. I was quite nervous as some of my friends told me stories of their interviews which included interrogation regarding everything in their paperwork, as well as questioning on points of law, somewhat similar to my interview with the Chief Assistant for my job. The day of my interview with the character committee member I again donned my best gray twenty-five-dollar suit and went to his office on Court Street in downtown Brooklyn which was the location of many law offices.

Upon my arrival at the office of the character committee member I told the receptionist my name and was told to have a seat. After waiting nervously for about ten minutes, I was ushered into the committee member's windowed office overlooking Court Street. He was a large man sitting behind a large desk. Without getting up or shaking hands, he somewhat curtly told me to take a seat. He began reading through my paperwork on his desk. As he thumbed through my file my anxiety increased, anticipating the worst in the way of interrogation, based upon the experiences of some of my friends over the previous few weeks, as well as his demeanor. After a couple of minutes, he looked up at me and said "ticket for going through a stop sign. Not much of a criminal record."

Then he smiled, stood up and reached out to shake my hand.

"Good luck to you Steven."

That was it, I was done. Not a single question about anything. I had gone through the character committee review unscathed.

A few weeks later I was given a date to report to the courthouse for swearing in as an attorney. Once I was admitted to practice, I was assigned to the Criminal Court. They started the new guys (there were a few women in the office, but it was mostly guys back then) in the "complaint room" of the criminal court. I don't know if this was a result of my interview performance or was something they had been doing for some time, but it was a good opportunity for an in-depth study of criminal law, as a step to learning how to handle cases in court. It also gave us an opportunity to interact with the police on a more informal basis, before being thrown into the more formal procedures in the courtroom. I will explain shortly what I meant by being "thrown" into the courtroom.

The workday in the complaint room involved each of us assigned there to sit in a cubicle with a typist (no desktop computers back then). There were weekday weekend and evening shifts, as the police were continually bringing defendants in for processing. Police officers, who had made an arrest and had deposited their prisoner downstairs, in a holding cell waiting to be arraigned before a judge and have bail set, would wait to be called in by one of the half dozen new assistant district attorneys working in the complaint room. In some cases, the officers would be accompanied by complaining witnesses who had been robbed, assaulted or had been otherwise victimized by the person accused of the criminal activity, who was awaiting arraignment.

Once the officer, and often the victim, were brought into our cubicle, the officer and complainant would tell us what happened. After listening to the story, and perhaps asking some questions to elicit additional details, we would search through a looseleaf copy of the New York State Penal Law which listed all criminal offenses. Next, we would pick out what sounded like the crimes that were committed. Then we would dictate to the typist, sitting next to us in the cubicle, a short description of what occurred and the sections of the Penal Law that we thought we could prove had been violated through the actions of the accused party or parties.

This would be typed on a form called a complaint, using carbon paper to produce multiple copies for the judge, the defense and our file. This was the charging document the judge would review in deciding whether to set bail as a requirement for release of the defendant being charged. In addition, the judge would set the date and the courtroom for the next court appearance.

One very unofficial challenge, among the newly minted assistant D.A.s, was to think of as many crimes as possible to charge. There would be somewhat of a daily contest for who had been able to come up with the most violations of the Penal Law to charge against an individual defendant, based upon what each defendant had done.

In the end our attempt at showing how smart we were did not matter, as most cases were reduced for plea bargaining purposes, or were felonies that ultimately went to the grand jury which would decide what crimes to actually charge against the defendant. For the purpose of the initial arraignment and the setting of bail, it made us novices feel like we were doing our job to punish the criminals by coming up with multiple crimes to charge, at least initially.

The paperwork would then be shipped down to the courtroom where the arraignments took place. The assistant D.A. in arraignments and the defense attorney would each get a "carbon copy" of the complaint form that was filed with the judge. The judge would then read the defendant the charges against him, or more often, to save time the defense attorney would waive reading the charges and the judge would determine whether to set bail and, if there was bail, how much.

Being in the D.A.s office led to many unusual experiences, both in and out of the office. The longer I worked there the more bizarre events occurred, some of which were merely a reflection of the times and others because of the very unusual circumstances in which we worked.

We frequently interacted with private security, so called "store detectives", from local stores, who had "arrested" people for shoplifting and came to the complaint room to provide the information for the arraignments. They did not wear uniforms, which allowed them to observe people in the stores, without being noticed.

On one occasion, while shopping at one of those stores, I suddenly realized that a private security person, with whom I had interacted a few times, was following me around the store. It occurred to me that he likely placed my face, but not where he had seen me before. Therefore, I must be a suspicious individual whom he had previously observed.

As a result, he apparently felt the need to follow me to be certain I did not steal anything. To see if my theory was correct (rather than simply going over and saying hello, as I was concerned it would alert people that he was security), I then began to walk from counter to counter lifting objects and examining them. The scrutiny I received from the security guard became more intense with each item I examined and put down, as he followed me closely from counter to counter. After a few minutes, I decided not to waste any more of his time and left the store, apparently much to his relief.

After spending a few weeks in the complaint room, I began to take a turn in the arraignment courtroom (each courtroom was assigned a number and referred to as a "Part"), between shifts in the complaint room. Due to the high crime rate, the arraignment Part went from nine in the morning until about eleven at night. Saturday night was particularly interesting as, for some reason, the more unusual criminal activities seemed to occur on Saturdays.

In addition, Saturday night was also an evening for cheap dates. We often had a full audience of couples watching us. On one Saturday, a friend of mine from college decided it would be fun to see me at work and have a cheap date. Therefore, he and his girlfriend brought my wife to watch the show. When I returned home later that evening my wife's only question was: "why did that police officer bring the bloody sword into the courtroom?"

I explained that I thought he was trying to emphasize how dangerous the guy who had used the sword to attack someone would be if he was let out. Therefore, the officer brought the sword into the courtroom and held it point down on the table in front of him while the defendant, in an equally bloody shirt, was being arraigned. The fact that the sword had dried blood on the blade only served to emphasize the police officer's perspective to the judge.

The volume of crime was so high in those days that we set all-time records for the number of felony indictments returned by the grand juries. As a result of the volume, the office had policies for reducing charges on certain felonies to misdemeanors or lower level felonies. This was done to have the resources available to prosecute the most serious crimes as felonies. The result was freeing the courts from holding trials on more minor matters that were still technically felonies, but not viewed, at least by the DA's office, as serious enough to charge as felonies. Certain felonies were therefore reduced to misdemeanors or lower-level felonies to alleviate the backlog of the more serious crimes awaiting trial.

Of course, the policies which were established in determining what was less serious and therefore should be reduced to avoid backlogs were very subjective determinations made on the administrative level in the office. One example, if you killed your brother or your girlfriend or someone else you had a close relationship with, you were generally not charged with murder, but the lesser crime of manslaughter. Both of those were felonies, however, the office had two special Parts (courtrooms) devoted solely to murder trials. With approximately 400 homicides in the county each year, there was concern about overloading the murder Parts and delaying those prosecutions. Therefore, a procedure was set up to reduce certain homicides from murder to manslaughter so that the murder Parts could move the "more serious" homicides, like killing strangers, or killing someone during a robbery, to trial more rapidly than would have occurred if all homicides were treated as murders. More on the details of this policy later.

Crimes other than homicides also had their own hierarchy of seriousness. If someone stole a car, unless it was a model from that year or the year before, it was charged as a misdemeanor, even though a felony grand larceny in those days was technically stealing something worth more than $250.00. Even a three year old car was worth more than $250 in the early 1970s. I can recall a funeral director whose three year old hearse had been stolen strenuously objecting to the misdemeanor plea I offered the thief. He noted the vehicle was worth thousands of dollars. I told him that was office policy despite the actual value of his hearse and there was nothing I could do except offer the plea to a misdemeanor.

Likewise, assaults had their own criteria for charging. Both assault in the first degree and assault in the second degree were felonies. One of the factors in determining whether to charge a serious assault as assault in the first degree or second degree was how many stitches were required to sew up the wound caused by the assault. There was nothing in the statutes that took the number of stitches into account. However, the office was so overwhelmed with these crimes that there had to be a policy in handling the charges.

On one occasion a squad of officers brought in eight prostitutes who had been arrested as part of an operation to clean up a particular neighborhood. At arraignment, I offered the group pleas to disorderly conduct, a substantial reduction of the charges that each faced. The offer was accepted. When we finished the Sargent in charge came up to me and asked what I was doing. I explained we had a lot more serious crimes to deal with and prosecuting the eight prostitutes, through the system would take more time than it was worth.

He looked at me and said: "I guess I shouldn't waste my time."

I noted: "there is probably some more serious stuff going on out there that you can spend your time addressing."

I also pointed out that among the eight prostitutes they had arrested that evening, the guy in drag was the best looking. Therefore, I concluded that it was unlikely they were doing a lot of business on the local streets. I suggested to the Sargent that more serious criminal activity might warrant attention, in that neighborhood.

As the assistant assigned to arraignments you had to make bail recommendations to the court and in some instances, where there were minor charges, like the group of prostitutes, you would work out a plea deal on the spot. We had to decide on a bail recommendation as we opened the file which we had not previously seen. There were also no real guidelines but generally we felt that being tough looked good to the bosses. This was long before the bail reform laws that have been adopted in recent years. Except for very minor actions by someone without much of a criminal record, some bail was requested by us and often set on most charges.

During one of my first days in arraignments, the Deputy Bureau Chief came down to watch me for a few minutes. Unfortunately for the two people arraigned during that time, I asked for nearly double the bail I might have otherwise requested. As a brand-new assistant, I was concerned the deputy chief watching what I was doing would think I was being too easy on the criminals if I asked for less bail. The next day he stopped in to see me.

"You were doing a nice job in arraignments yesterday."

"Thank you."

"My only criticism would be that you were a bit high on the bail requests."

Early on, I had a case where the defense attorney stated he needed a longer adjournment than the judge was proposing. Usually, cases were set for further action within a week or less of the arraignment. The defense attorney explained to the judge that he needed the additional time because "Mr. Green is not currently available."

I did not recall anything about Mr. Green related to this case. I quickly looked at the file again. My recollection was confirmed, there was no reference to a Mr. Green having anything to do with the case. I objected to the adjournment request.

"Your honor, there is no Mr. Green involved in this case. I see no reason for the delay for a fictitious Mr. Green."

The judge looked down, frowned at me and shook his head. Then he called me and the defense attorney up for a discussion at the bench, out of the hearing of the others in the courtroom. The judge looked down at me with a grim expression on his face.

"Son, when he said Mr. Green is not available, he meant he has not yet been paid. He needs time for his client to come up with his fee. I will grant the requested adjournment."

Here was another practical pointer in criminal law practice which was not covered in law school or our training in the DA's office. Each new court appearance was a learning experience about the practicalities of practicing criminal law in New York City in the 1970s.

Often, the defendants' friends or relatives would appear at the arraignment. They often took offense at requests for bail, knowing that this would often result in the defendant remaining in jail awaiting further proceedings. This resulted in the friends and relatives of the accused standing behind the railing separating the attorneys from the courtroom spectators and whispering threats to "get" the assistant DA after court. These threats were particularly prevalent during night court. Therefore, when I left the courthouse to walk to my car at about 11 P.M., I often asked one of the court officers to escort me to my car. There was no staff parking lot and I often had to park my car two or three blocks away from the courthouse.

One court officer, Charlie, was a former bodyguard for the Haitian Dictator, Papa Doc Duvalier. Charlie was about six foot six and quite an imposing figure. He indicated early in my assignment to night arraignments that he thought it was only proper that I be escorted.

Charlie had a very direct approach to any possible threat. Generally, one of the court officers was designated at the end of the court session to make a night deposit of bail money. This would be at a bank a few blocks from the courthouse that had a night deposit box. If Charlie was assigned on a particular night to make the deposit, he pulled his gun and held it pointing up, at shoulder height, as he left the courthouse. Anyone intending to approach him would have no misunderstanding as to Charlie's intentions, should they try to interfere with his official duties.

There was another court officer, Jack, whom I learned lived not far from me. Whenever I was assigned to night court and Jack was on duty, I generously offered to drive him and his gun home. My "generosity" resulted in my having an armed escort on the walk to my car and the ride home.

If a prisoner became violent during the arraignment, this could result in them being lifted and carried out of the courtroom. Sometimes, opening the door to the holding cells was accomplished, as the court officers struggled with the prisoner, by using his head as a battering ram. No one seemed to think anything of it. These activities were merely part of the day-to-day procedures in the arraignment courtroom.

On one occasion a brawl broke out between relatives of a prisoner and the relatives of the person he had allegedly assaulted. As a result of the brawl, the court officers escorted me and the judge into an area behind the courtroom. There was a running battle in the courtroom, in the hallways and up and down the stairs for about half an hour before all of the combatants were arrested and order restored.

Occasionally, a judge would do something that was even unusual for the arraignment Part. One day a young man was being arraigned for painting graffiti on a subway car. As he stood before the judge, we all noticed the prisoner was wearing a quite expensive looking leather jacket. The judge looked down over his glasses and instructed the young man to hand up his jacket. The young fellow looked a bit startled but did as he was instructed and handed his jacket to a court officer. The court officer brought the jacket over to the judge who again looked down. But now the Judge was holding an ink stamp in his hand and said:

"Do you see this stamp, I have in my hand?"

The young fellow looking concerned, nodded and said:

"Yes, Judge."

"I think I would like to use this stamp, that has my name on it, to stamp my name all over your jacket."

Looking terrified, the defendant said, "Please don't."

"Well young man, if you don't think it is right for me to stamp my name all over your jacket, why do you think it is OK for you to spray paint your name all over a subway car?"

Glancing down at the floor he mumbled, "It isn't right."

"Correct. Now take back your jacket. I am going to release you without any requirement for bail, come back next Monday and don't do it again."

Watching the little melodrama seemed to be an unusual but not unreasonable practical lesson for the young fellow, who hopefully got the point.

The arraignment Part was not always limited to mundane requests for bail.

One Saturday, some detectives appeared requesting that the judge issue a search warrant involving some pornographic movies that they suspected were being stored at a particular location. The definition of pornography was stricter in those days, than it is now, with nudity and sexual content being more prevalent in current movies. The detectives had a sample movie to use, as their proof of "probable cause" that there was pornographic material and therefore a search warrant should be issued by the judge.

The judge instructed me to follow him into a room behind the courtroom where the police officers seeking the search warrant were waiting. I had no idea why I needed to be there, since I had nothing to do with the issuance of a search warrant. But the judge specifically directed me to accompany him to the room where, unbeknownst to me, they were setting up a movie projector to play an allegedly pornographic film. I felt uncomfortable but I needed to obey the direct order of the judge. I, along with the court reporter, and as many court officers as could manage to squeeze themselves into the room, where they apparently knew what was about to happen, were then all subjected, or in some cases pleased to observe, the showing of the movie.

Although, I do not believe all the court officers had been directed by the judge to squeeze into the small room, I suspect they felt it was their duty to protect the judge from an untoward incident by being as close to him as possible while the pornographic movie was being shown.

It was quite a strange experience. The judge narrated the silent film, describing the actions in graphic detail for the court reporter to take down, apparently in order to justify issuing the search warrant. He began by describing, in some detail, a bedroom with a naked woman on the bed. He then made a statement for the record, that I still remember more than fifty years later.

"A penis has now appeared in the foreground, moving toward the woman."

He went on, for longer than it seemed necessary, allowing the obviously pornographic movie to run, while describing in great detail the activities taking place in the film, to prove that there was pornographic material involved. Finally, after what seemed an eternity, he completed his narration and issued the warrant. This was not what I expected to be a portion of the duties of covering arraignments on a Saturday in criminal court. Although, it provided a good story to tell the other assistant district attorneys the following week, some of whom were displeased that they had not been assigned to arraignments that Saturday.

Every corner of the courthouse had its own peculiarities going on day and night. Even the courthouse elevator operators had their own strange and unusual habits. The building was built in the 1930s with funding from the Works Project Administration (WPA) to provide projects and jobs during the Great Depression. When I began working in the courthouse it still did not have automatic elevators. Therefore, each one of several elevators had an operator who stopped on the requested floors. One very flamboyant female elevator operator was known for her standard response to anyone asking if she was going down. The elevator would stop at a floor and an uninitiated prospective passenger would innocently say:

"Are you going down?"

Invariably, her response was:

"Ladies do not go down. However, we are descending."

Those of us who were regulars continued to look forward to the inevitable question, "are you going down" and her response. We all knew better than to phrase the question in a manner that would elicit her response that ladies do not go down. We all became indoctrinated into asking her if she was descending which would bring a smile to her face, as she saw that she had taught us the proper manner of addressing the "lady" operating the elevator.

4

CHAPTER 4
"ALL PURPOSE" CRIMINAL COUTROOMS"

Working as an Assistant District Attorney in Criminal Court was nothing like the depiction of criminal proceedings we constantly see on television.

After a few weeks of experience in arraignments, my next assignment was to handle one of the "all purpose" courtrooms in the courthouse. They were called all-purpose because they handled all aspects of misdemeanor prosecutions including hearings and non-jury trials as well as felony hearings, to see if the cases in which felonies were charged should be held over for the grand jury for indictment. Once a case was sent to the grand jury, if an indictment was issued, the case was transferred to the State Supreme Court for further processing and potentially a trial.

The felony hearings in criminal court were supposed to take place within three business days of arraignment if the prisoner had not been released on bail. The defense attorneys took advantage of the felony hearings to cross-examine the witnesses to get a head start on potential defense strategies. The prosecutors tried to limit the number of witnesses brought in to testify to the bare minimum needed to demonstrate "probably cause" to hold the case for grand jury action.

The limited nature of the felony hearing did not come close to approaching the requirement of proof beyond a reasonable doubt required for a criminal trial. Therefore, we attempted to avoid giving the defense attorneys an additional opportunity to cross-examine more witnesses than were needed for the limited purpose of proving probable cause in the felony hearing.

Generally, the calendar in each courtroom was about seventy cases each day. All of us assigned to courtrooms would appear at the office of the District Attorney's criminal court bureau each morning. We were given the calendar (the list of cases) and files, for each day, for the first time, at 9 in the morning. Unless there was a case I had handled a day or two before that had been adjourned for a witness to appear or adjourned at the request of the defendant's attorney, in most instances I had never seen the file before it was handed to me that day at 9 a.m.

Therefore, as a general rule, each file was totally new to me when I received it each morning half an hour before the call of the calendar starting at 9:30. As a result, I had just enough time to glance at the calendar handed to me along with the files, perhaps opening a few of the files before getting myself to the courtroom, so that I would be ready when the judge called the cases at 9:30.

Being late for the start of the calendar call was not an option. Not being present before the judge entered the courtroom would put the judge in a bad mood. The judge's bad mood would generally carry on for the rest of the day and cause the judge to take out his annoyance on the latecomer at any opportunity that arose during the day.

Each file had one of those complaint forms on top. As the cases were called by the court clerk, I would be allowed about 15 seconds to glace at the file while the police officer and/or witnesses came up to the front of the courtroom. The judge would then ask if I was ready to proceed with the hearing or nonjury trial.

Basically, as I had not had a chance to actually study the file, I would turn to whomever came up when the case was called and ask, "do we have everyone here?" If I was told everyone I needed was there, I would tell the judge I was ready to proceed with the hearing or trial, although I still knew nothing more about the case than the summary in the criminal complaint form. If someone necessary to the proceeding was missing, and the officer who came up remembered to tell me before I said I was ready, I would tell the judge I needed an adjournment.

Since we were usually moved to different courtrooms each week, if a case had been adjourned previously that adjournment may have been at the request of the assistant who was in that courtroom the week before. In the event the case had already been adjourned by the prosecutor on a previous occasion there was a good chance, if we requested another adjournment, the judge would dismiss the case, or if the defendant was being held on bail, at the very least, he would be released from custody.

Opening the file for the first time as the case was called, it was particularly difficult to object to the dismissal if someone else had been covering that courtroom the week before. Suddenly you had cases dismissed not because of anything you had done, but because of previous adjournments due to another assistant DA being unprepared.

Sometimes, if a matter seemed to involve a minor offense, or if it had been on the calendar before and a witness was still missing, likely resulting in a dismissal, I would offer a plea deal on the spot to the defense attorney. However, if I was ready to proceed with the hearing the judge would mark the case for "second call" and then call the next case to see if the next case was ready.

Telling the judge you were "ready" to proceed with the felony hearing or non-jury trial on a particular matter meant you hoped all the parties for the proceeding were really there and that you would get enough time when the case was called again to figure out what it was about.

Of course, not having had an opportunity to thoroughly review the file yet, I had to rely on the officer who came up saying that everyone I needed was present. On a few occasions, I was advised that everyone I needed was there. Then I found out when the case was called for the hearing that someone was missing. Luckily, that did not happen too often as the judges were not at all pleased when that situation arose.

Over the course of about an hour the judge would go through the entire list of cases for that day. Then the judge would begin calling the cases that had been marked ready, during the first call of the calendar, to start the hearings and nonjury trials. As the judge would call the first hearing, the process would go something like this:

Judge: "Are you ready?"

Me: "May I have just a moment to speak with the officer?"

Judge: "Make it quick."

I would quickly turn to the officer and ask what the case was about and within about 30 seconds the judge would tell me my time was up and I should call my first witness.

My training for this intense process had consisted of being in a courtroom for one week with another assistant, who had at most a few more months of experience. After that first week I was on my own, without my "mentor" to guide me.

On my very first day alone in that courtroom I had a hearing scheduled to determine whether evidence was to be suppressed, due to a claimed illegal search. Although I understood the basic legal issues involved in what constituted a "legal" search, I had only a vague idea of what went on at such a hearing. I had no advance warning about the case. To add to my panic, I had never seen such an evidentiary hearing conducted. Not to mention, it was my very first day alone in a courtroom handling any hearings.

During a short break between the calendar being called and starting the hearings, I ran out in the hall to find the guy who had "trained" me the week before. I found him and explained I had to conduct a hearing to determine whether evidence should be suppressed and had never seen one done.

Then to make me feel even more secure he responded: "I have never seen one either, I will come in and watch you do it."

Somehow, that did not make me feel more confident about doing the hearing. I had to do the hearing and there was not enough time to find someone else from the DA's office who could give me any guidance. I managed to muddle through and defeat the request to exclude the evidence. I assumed after that my handling of the hearing was a model for the process, at least for my former instructor who had observed it.

It appeared that the attorneys working for the Legal Aid Society representing indigent defendants were as overwhelmed as we were. One morning we had a defendant, who was being held on bail, charged with petty larceny. He did not have a record of prior arrests. I offered his Legal Aid attorney a plea bargain involving a misdemeanor charge and thirty days in jail. The defendant took the plea and was taken out to the holding area.

About half an hour later the same Legal Aid attorney had another client brought in from the holding area. This defendant happened to have the same name as the fellow who had earlier pleaded guilty to the misdemeanor charge. This man was charged with armed robbery, a serious felony offense. When we started discussing the charges the defendant objected that he was only there on a petty larceny charge. The judge asked his birth date and the date he gave did not match the date on the armed robbery file but did match the birth date on the petty larceny file.

He was brought back to the holding area and the first fellow who had pleaded guilty to the petty larceny charge was brought back out. He was asked his birth date, and it was the same as the man who was charged with the felony armed robbery. He also acknowledged that he was facing a charge of armed robbery. He was questioned why he had pled guilty to the misdemeanor charge which had nothing to do with the accusations against him. He responded that it was a good deal, so he took it.

This resulted in our having to undo the original plea and start over with the two men. The fellow who was actually charged with the petty larceny refused the plea I had offered. Apparently, he did not view it as a particularly "good deal".

The assistants assigned to the criminal court would be moved to different courtrooms and judges weekly. Sometimes we would be assigned to a courtroom by ourselves or sometimes be assigned along with another assistant. Once when I was assigned to a courtroom with another assistant, on a particular morning we discovered we had one defendant who had 21 cases of his own on our calendar that day.

In going over the charges against him, we realized that each time he was arrested he had given the police a different date of birth. Even though his fingerprints were taken, apparently no one had bothered to check his prints against the database. As a result of his providing a different date of birth each time he was arrested he was let out on bail, because the name and birth date he provided did match any record of any prior arrests in the database. In addition, each time he was arrested and released he also failed to return to court on his next court date.

Finally, with his most recent arrest, someone bothered to check his fingerprints against those in the database. Suddenly the police realized he had been arrested and let out on bail on ten previous occasions. As a result, that day we had eleven different cases involving his ten prior arrests plus his most recent arrest. In addition, the assistant in the complaint room, following the process of coming up with as many crimes as possible to charge, had added ten charges of bail jumping related to his ten prior arrests and his failure to appear for further proceedings on those previous charges.

In reviewing the cases, we determined they were all relatively petty. Some were technically felonies, but each one taken by itself would have been a case that probably would have been reduced to a misdemeanor plea with a fine or at most a couple of months in prison. If he had taken a plea when he was first arrested and, for example, had been sentenced to thirty days in jail, once he was arrested again the office might have sought a slightly longer jail time due to his repeat offense.

Yet, even then, due to the backlog of serious felonies in the office, he likely would have been offered pleas to misdemeanors. The criminal court had authority to sentence someone to a maximum of two one-year consecutive sentences in prison for two "A" misdemeanors, for example petty larceny, the highest form of misdemeanor.

After reviewing all the cases, I suggested to my partner in the courtroom that we offer a plea to two "A" misdemeanors, to be served in two consecutive one-year sentences. I proposed the plea to the two "A" misdemeanors of petty larceny should be used to satisfy all the charges. In that way, the office could avoid taking months of time, and the potential of multiple trials, prosecuting all 21 rather minor charges.

My partner was not happy with my suggestion and said, "that is nuts, he has 21 cases several felonies and we will get in trouble if we do what you are suggesting."

I said, "look most of the cases are petty and if they came in as individual charges we would reduce them to misdemeanors and probably ask for at most 60 to 90 days in jail in each case. We can clear this entire calendar in a morning and not take up weeks or even months of time prosecuting these cases."

"If you want to make this deal, go ahead, but I am leaving the courtroom if you plan on going ahead. I do not want to have anything to do with this crazy scheme. You can tell the boss it was all your doing."

After he left, I suggested to the judge that I would like to conference with defense counsel to see if we could work something out. The judge was happy to see if we could clear that mess off his calendar. I offered the defense attorney the plea deal I had discussed with my now absent partner. After speaking with his client, the attorney advised his client would accept the proposed deal and agree to the two consecutive one year sentences on the two misdemeanors.

The defense attorney and I spoke to the judge, who was delighted to clear his calendar and he agreed to the proposed sentence. Within about twenty minutes we cleared all twenty-one of the cases on the calendar, which involved that defendant.

The next morning, I was called into the office of the chief of the criminal court bureau. I was nervous. He rarely called anyone in, except to yell at them for messing up. I thought for sure my courtroom partner had correctly predicted that I would be punished for clearing all those cases by taking the pleas to just two misdemeanors. I nervously entered his office.

"You wanted to see me?"

"Steve, I saw what you did yesterday with the fellow with the 21 cases."

Feeling the need to justify my actions, I replied:

"I felt they were mostly petty crimes and it seemed like they would take up an inordinate amount of time if we went ahead with them individually."

"I agree. Nice job clearing the calendar of all that garbage."

This was my first lesson, that taking some initiative was not a bad idea and would be acknowledged by the superiors in the office.

5

CHAPTER 5
JUDGE CABLE

Judge Cable, a large man, about six feet tall and about fifty years old with greying hair, had one of the busiest courtrooms in the courthouse. The problem the attorneys appearing before him had was that he operated by his own rules and did some peculiar things. Therefore, it was difficult to predict what would happen on any particular day, plus his rules changed with his moods.

To him, the basic rules of criminal procedure, like what constituted hearsay testimony that would not be admissible, appeared to be merely suggestions that he could, and often did, ignore. Moreover, he had his own somewhat unusual perspective of what constituted justice. As a result, those appearing before him had no idea what to expect from day to day, except that something unexpected would likely occur.

Even though assignments to a particular courtroom and judge were generally for a week, the assistant DAs assigned to him each week rarely made it through a full five days. Cable would do something totally unheard of that violated some rule or custom of court procedure and the assistant assigned that week would begin arguing with him. Cable had little tolerance for objections to his actions, even if his actions were completely inconsistent with established norms, or even the law.

Usually, by a Wednesday afternoon the chief of the criminal court bureau would get a phone call from Judge Cable demanding that the assistant assigned for that week be removed from his courtroom, upon threat of the assistant being held in contempt of court. As a result, the assistant would be removed and someone else sent in to finish out the week. Sometimes the attorney who had acted as the substitute would also be assigned the following week as well. But ultimately the substitute would suffer the same fate as his predecessor, as no one seemed able to get through an assignment for more than three days in Judge Cable's courtroom.

Assignment to Cable's courtroom was what some would imagine purgatory must be like and was clearly known to be the worst assignment in the courthouse. Everyone dreaded being assigned to him, due to his erratic behavior, threats of contempt citations and his general mistreatment of the assistants assigned to his courtroom.

On Friday afternoons our assignments for the following week would be posted in the office. Each week I would hold my breath, when I checked the assignments for the next week, hoping that I had not been unlucky enough to be assigned to Cable. Inevitably, after a few months in the criminal court, it became my turn to deal with Cable for a week.

I soon figured out that one of Cable's pet peeves was scheduling hearings and then not having the police officer or witness show up. So, after court each day I began calling the police officers and witnesses scheduled for the next day to remind them to attend. That worked most of the time. As a result, I had very few instances where the necessary parties did not appear for a scheduled hearing. In addition, if it turned out that we had scheduled a hearing for a day when the arresting officer was off duty, since I made the follow up calls, I was able to advise Cable that the officer was off duty that day and therefore unavailable. Generally, although not always, being able to give a reasonable explanation for the police officer's absence would keep Cable from blowing up at me.

As I already mentioned, Cable also tended to follow his own rules of procedure. They were often minor breaches of technicalities. I figured out that if it was not an important breach of the rules and most importantly his actions did not prejudice my case, it was not worth arguing about, as he would just get angry and do it anyway. As a result of my tolerating his idiosyncrasies, I apparently set the all-time world record by making it through an entire week without a call by Cable to the bureau chief to get me out of there.

On the next Friday afternoon, relieved that I had managed to make it through the entire week with Cable and would be able to move on to a more normal assignment the following week, I rushed to check the assignments for the following week. As my reward for not being banned from Judge Cable's courtroom, I was assigned to him the following week.

I again made it through the full week and felt assured, as rarely was anyone assigned to a particular judge for more than even a week, that I would finally receive a reprieve. Yet, the next week, the week after that and so on for a total of six weeks in a row I continued my assignment in Cable's courtroom. However, my real reward, after six weeks in purgatory, was a promotion. I guess, having been one of the few to survive Cable, they felt I knew what I was doing.

Yet, during those six weeks, I did have some interesting situations dealing with the Judge that persist as clear memories decades later. One day, while conducting a hearing, my police officer witness started to testify as to the contents of a radio call he received while on patrol.

"I received a radio call that a man fitting the defendant's description...."

The defense attorney, who Judge Cable did not like, interrupted by jumping up and objecting that by testifying to certain details of what the officer had been told on the radio call the officer was violating the hearsay rule which precluded someone testifying to what a third party, other than the defendant, had said. The attorney therefore argued the statement was not admissible.

Hearsay, in this case, would be a violation of a rule of evidence that does not permit the police officer to testify regarding information he heard from a radio dispatcher, who was relaying details of the alleged crime they had heard from yet another person. Under actual rules of evidence this would be a form of hearsay evidence and would not be admissible in a hearing before a normal judge.

"Counsel, your objection is overruled."

"Your, honor, on what basis are you overruling my objection, this testimony is clearly hearsay."

The Judge could not acknowledge that he overruled the objection because he did not like the defense attorney. Instead, Judge Cable, consistent with his inclination to make up the rules as he went along, cited "the police exception to the hearsay rule" as the basis for overruling the attorney's objection to the testimony about the radio call the police officer had begun to recite.

Of course, there is no such thing as a police exception to the hearsay rule. However, technicalities, like the actual law, never interfered with Judge Cable's rulings, especially if he did not like the attorney he was ruling against. Therefore, the exchange continued.

"Your honor, what police exception to the hearsay rule?"

"Counsel, sit down and be quiet."

Clearly, being on Cable's bad side had real world consequences for defense attorneys, as well as the prosecutors. We finished the felony hearing and the case was held over for the grand jury to act on the charges against the attorney's unfortunate client.

Later that same day, we had a hearing with a different defense attorney. In that hearing another police officer witness, began to also recite the content of a radio call that he had received on the night of the crime. The attorney jumped up objecting that the statement the officer was making was in violation of the hearsay rule.

Apparently Judge Cable did not have it in for that defense attorney and Judge Cable correctly sustained the objection to the hearsay testimony by the police officer. By sustaining the objection the Judge therefore correctly, unlike his allowing the officer in the earlier hearing to violate the hearsay rule, did not permit the police officer to testify about the specific details of third party information he had received during the radio call on the night of the incident.

At that point, since the Judge had made a contrary ruling just that morning, feeling more comfortable with the Judge, after surviving a couple of weeks assigned to him, and naturally being a bit of a wise guy under ordinary circumstances, I could not resist the opportunity to raise the issue for the judge. I stood up and said "your honor but what about the police exception to the hearsay rule?"

The defense attorney, who had not been there earlier in the day, was incredulous and immediately, with a look of confusion on his face, asked what I was talking about.

"What police exception to the hearsay rule your honor, I am unaware of any such exception?"

Of course, there was no such thing as a police exception to the hearsay rule. The Judge clearly knew I was indirectly, but politely without mentioning his earlier ruling, calling him out. He paused for a few seconds and then the Judge looked down at me, with a very slight smirk on his face, realizing full well what I was doing.

"Cowabonga, counsel. The district attorney will please sit down, the objection of defense counsel is sustained."

One morning we had a local activist who, along with his co-defendant, was charged with murder and was being held in custody. His case was on our calendar for a felony hearing to determine if the case should be held for grand jury action. The defendant, as was the practice in murder cases, was currently being held without bail. The office policy was to not hold felony hearings on murder cases, to avoid giving defense counsel an extra chance to cross-examine witnesses during a hearing on these serious cases.

The policy was to put the case directly into the grand jury and obtain an indictment, while the perpetrator was being held without bail in the lower criminal court. Yet, the law required that bail be set, if the indictment had not been handed down within three days of the perpetrator being placed into custody without the benefit of being released on bail. Otherwise, someone could be held indefinitely without the benefit of either a felony hearing on the charge or an indictment.

That morning the three days after initially being held without bail expired and the indictment had not yet been handed down. We had a telephone in the courtroom at the prosecutor's table, that would blink a light if a call was coming in, so as not to disrupt proceedings with a telephone ringing. Since, as was typical, I had no idea this case was on my calendar until I arrived in Judge Cable's courtroom, I called up to the office and asked what was happening.

A short time after, I received a call back that the case was being presented to the grand jury that morning. I was instructed to see if I could delay the case while it was still on the calendar in my courtroom until the afternoon, to allow for the indictment to be handed down. The issuance of the indictment would remove jurisdiction of the criminal court and Judge Cable and cause the case to be removed to State Supreme Court for further processing.

When the case was called, I advised Judge Cable.

"Your, honor, this matter is before the grand jury this morning and we expect a decision before lunch. We are requesting an adjournment until after the lunch break, in order to give the grand jury an opportunity to act on the matter."

The defense attorney objected, requesting that bail be set, as this was the third day since the defendant's arraignment on the charges. The Judge, to my surprise, agreed to hold the case until after the lunch break. I was relieved as I fully expected the indictment to be issued which would cause the defendant to be transferred to the Supreme Court later in the morning and that I would not see the case again.

Once the grand jury handed down an indictment the case is automatically transferred from the Criminal Court to the State Supreme Court for trial and no further action by the criminal court is required or permitted. Therefore, the expected indictment would preclude any action by Judge Cable and the matter would be off his calendar.

We did the rest of the calendar as usual that morning and then took a break for lunch. When I arrived back in the courtroom after lunch, the courtroom was packed with supporters of the defendant. There were so many people there they were standing on windowsills and inside the area, at the front of the courtroom, that is used to separate observers from the attorneys and the judge.

Apparently Judge Cable had some sympathy for this activist and his local politician attorney as the judge permitted a complete breakdown of courtroom decorum. The court officers took no action to move the people behind the railing that was supposed to separate the public from the court proceeding. As a result, I was basically surrounded by supporters of the defendant. In fact, the matter was covered by the local news which reported the next day that there were approximately 500 people within the courtroom, surrounding the "young assistant DA."

Before the judge entered the courtroom, I called up to the office again. I was advised the grand jury had voted the indictment. However, in order for the indictment to be official, it had to be signed by a Supreme Court Justice. Of course, as most of the court personnel were just coming back from lunch break, they had to find a judge to sign the indictment. I was told to stall as they were in process of getting it signed and would have a police officer bring it immediately to the criminal court to take the defendant into custody for the purpose of being arraigned before a Supreme Court Justice.

Judge Cable came out. "Well, counsel do you have an indictment with respect to this defendant?"

"Your honor, I have been advised the grand jury has voted an indictment for murder and the indictment is presently being signed by a justice of the Supreme Court. We expect it will be delivered here within less than half an hour. I request that the matter be held over for an additional half hour."

"Counsel, I gave you until after lunch. It is now after lunch. I am not giving you additional time as there is no indictment before me."

"Your honor, I have been advised the indictment has been voted on by the grand jury, the signature by a justice is a formality. The defendant is accused of a brutal murder and has now been formally indicted on that charge. He should not be released, until he is arraigned on the indictment and a justice of the Supreme Court determines the level of bail required to ensure his return and to protect the community."

"God damn it, counsel, do not instruct me on the procedures to be followed. You had all morning to come up with something and now you want more time. Bail is set at three thousand dollars."

Three thousand dollars bail on a murder was minimal, even fifty years ago. The Judge then slammed down his gavel, got up and walked out of the courtroom. To my amazement, and in further breach of all decorum, the defense attorney placed his hat upside down on the defense table and the members of the crowd began walking up. As they reached the defense table, they began dropping money in the hat to pay for the bail.

As the defendant's supporters streamed by me dropping five, ten, and twenty-dollar bills into the attorney's hat, I called up to the office again. I advised what was going on and told them to get someone there with the indictment as quickly as possible, before the defendant was released. There was real concern, based upon the nature of the crime, there could be further repercussions in that community, or he might even be a flight risk.

A short time later, while the paperwork was still being processed in the criminal court, the defendant was rearrested under the indictment, was arraigned before a Supreme Court justice and held without bail, pending trial on his murder indictment. There was no question in my mind that only in Judge Cable's courtroom could such a circus-like atmosphere prevail.

Judge Cable's antics continued on an almost daily basis. On another occasion, we had a nonjury trial with Judge Cable presiding. The defendant was accused of pulling a gun on some other men. The charge was menacing, a misdemeanor, as he did have a license for the gun he allegedly used. Five men testified as to the details of the crime. Each witness reiterated that the defendant had threatened the people in question with a gun, which clearly met the legal criteria for a charge of misdemeanor menacing. Their stories were detailed and consistent and the defense attorney, despite a valiant effort, did nothing to undermine their consistent testimony concerning the defendant's actions.

The defendant did not testify which, while not required and perfectly within the defendant's right, would by itself ordinarily raise a question as to the defendant's innocence. The general theory is if he were innocent, why would he not deny the claims by the others as to what happened? Defense counsel instead called the defendant's wife to the stand.

As he called her, I turned and an attractive young woman, wearing a short skirt and a very tight-fitting and lowcut sweater over her very large breasts, walked to the witness stand. As she took the oath to tell the truth, she leaned forward slightly toward the judge so that he could get a full view of her cleavage, revealed by her lowcut sweater.

Not surprisingly, her testimony was completely at odds with that of the other witnesses. She claimed to be a witness to the entire event. She claimed that everything testified to by the other witnesses was all a lie and that her husband had done nothing.

I carefully cross-examined her, poking holes in her story, even getting her to admit that, because she loved her husband, she would even be willing to lie for him. I felt that between the testimony of multiple witnesses and my cross examination of the defendant's obviously prejudiced wife, I had a strong case for conviction.

At the close of the case, Judge Cable took less than a minute to consider his verdict in the case and found the man not guilty of the charges against him.

As it was the end of the day, when we adjourned after that nonjury trial, I followed the Judge into his chambers behind the courtroom. I asked him if I could speak with him. I was outraged at the result of the trial. I felt I had to say something but also knew I had to be diplomatic in my approach, or I would suffer the usual consequences of his wrath. Although, at that point after several weeks of assignment to his courtroom, being thrown out might have been a preferable result. Yet, there was no appeal available to the prosecution and getting him angry at me would serve no constructive purpose.

"Judge, I am a relatively new lawyer and have not done a lot of trial work. I thought I had a strong case with the five witnesses. Plus, I thought I showed some serious inconsistencies in the wife's testimony, along with her obvious prejudice in favor of her husband. As I am just learning how to try cases, I was hoping you could explain where I made errors, so I could learn from the experience and hopefully not make the same mistakes again."

The Judge stood up from behind his desk with a big smile on his face. I was not sure what to expect as he came toward me. When he reached me, he was just below my six-foot two height. He put his arm around my shoulder and said: "son, you have to have the good-looking women on your side." That was all he said.

Not another word was uttered about the case, the evidence or my cross examination of the wife. Just have the good-looking women on your side when you are trying a case. I said nothing further. What could I say? I thanked him for the advice and left.

Another lesson in the practicalities of practicing criminal law in New York City in the 1970s that was not taught as part of the course curriculum in law school.

6

CHAPTER 6
I FINALLY ESCAPED FROM JUDGE CABLE

Immediately before my promotion, apparently as a result of my surviving six weeks with Judge Cable, I was assigned to one of two courtrooms that conducted misdemeanor jury trials in the criminal court. It was good experience selecting and trying cases before a jury. I lost my first jury trial to an attorney who was a former assistant DA and had years of experience trying cases before juries.

After the jury issued its decision, the judge, who was one of the more senior jurists in the Courthouse, called me into his chambers and was kind enough to point out a few mistakes I had made in my cross examination of the defendant.

"Steve, you did a generally good job, but your cross examination of the defendant fell a little short of the mark. You managed to get him to acknowledge certain things that opened the door for you. But, at that point you stopped your cross examination. When your questions open a door, drive a truck through that door and keep on going."

"Thank you, your honor, I will keep that in mind."

I guess I caught on as I won the second jury trial.

Yet again the unusual office procedures came to light. For the trial I had three witnesses scheduled to testify. The office procedure was to request two dollars for each witness to cover their expenses (subway and bus fare was twenty-five cents). Before the trial started, I went to the office of the Comptroller for the DA's office and requisitioned six dollars to give to my three trial witnesses when they appeared to testify. Although the trial went well, one of the witnesses I had intended to call to testify never showed up. When the trial was over, I went back to the office of the comptroller to return the two dollars that had not been used for the witness who failed to appear.

I entered the office and advised the woman at the front desk I had two dollars that had not been used by a witness, as the witness had not appeared for trial. I explained that I wished to return the two dollars. She took two dollars from me and asked me to have a seat in the waiting area.

During roughly the next half an hour I watched people scurrying in and out of offices and conferring with each other in whispers. Finally, the young woman returned with a receipt for the return of the two dollars I had given her.

Then she said: "The Comptroller would like to see you." She led me to his office and closed the door. I was told to have a seat. And then the Comptroller began to speak to me.

"Steve, my staff just spent half an hour entering the return of a two-dollar witness fee." Then in a raised voice he said: "if that ever happens again, just keep the two dollars. We spent more than two dollars' worth of time processing the paperwork."

Of course, being a novice, I had thought; if I do not use the fee I should return it. Also, I was concerned that if I did not return the fee and someone found out a witness had not appeared, I would be in trouble for not returning the two dollars. How was I to know that, apparently in the history of the DA's office no witness had ever before failed to appear, and therefore no assistant DA had ever had to return a witness fee. As a result, there was no procedure in place for such a contingency until I had returned the two dollars that day.

Shortly after completing my two jury trials, I was "promoted" to the position of the "number three" person in the criminal court bureau. I was number 3 behind the chief and deputy chief of the criminal court bureau. I was put in charge of various administrative duties, including certain aspects of scheduling and making sure the courtrooms were all covered by an appropriate number of assistant district attorneys, depending on the size of the regular calendars in each courtroom. There was no salary increase and I had no real authority over anyone, but other than the bureau chief and deputy chief, the so called "third man" was the only assistant working in the office at the criminal court.

Continuing in the surreal system of training for work in the office, I spent a week with the guy I was replacing. One thing that came up with some frequency was the issue of releasing cars that had been seized by the police, most often in relation to drug possession arrests.

If the charges were ultimately dropped, in most instances the car would be released to the owner. The position of third man involved handling the paperwork required for the police department to release the car. Therefore, I asked what I thought was a somewhat logical question, related to the duties of my new position. I asked my predecessor when a car should or should not be released.

The guy I was replacing shrugged his shoulders and said: "if you are not sure don't release it."

I asked: "what happens then?"

"Then they can sue the city and a judge will decide if they are entitled to the car. Don't stress over it."

He provided no further information or guidance on the issue. Procedural detail was not a hallmark of the processes in the office. Aside from a couple of bomb scares, which gave me a chance to stay behind to catch up on paperwork while others were evacuated from the courthouse (I was young and not too bright), nothing particularly interesting happened while I held that position. After a couple of months in that position it was time for me to move on to another bureau in the office.

7

CHAPTER 7
MY NEXT ASSIGNMENT

After a stint in the criminal court most of the assistants were promoted to the grand jury bureau. It was there that the various felony complaints, other than homicides, were presented by the members of that bureau to the grand juries to determine if the charges should result in indictment. Homicides were presented to the grand jury by members of a special homicide bureau. After an indictment was issued by a grand jury the case was transferred to the State Supreme Court which is a trial court. In the Supreme Court either plea deals were worked out or the case was held over for trial.

The appointment of an assistant D.A. to the Grand Jury Bureau was the step before assignment, in most instances, to a courtroom in the State Supreme Court, where the assistants assigned to the various courtrooms handled the felonies. Each assistant had somewhat limited authority to reduce charges in order to make plea deals and if no plea could be worked out then the case would go to trial. Some assistants were tougher than others and would therefore end up having more trials, as the defense attorneys did not think the plea deals offered were fair.

The Homicide and Investigations Bureau was a parallel assignment to the grand jury bureau. Homicide and Investigations was reserved for assistants who handled the investigation of homicides and presented just those cases to the grand jury, along with conducting investigations into police transgressions.

While most assistants went from criminal court to the grand jury bureau, there were only a total of eight at a time assigned to homicide and investigations, in addition to the chief and deputy chief of the bureau. Those eight were handpicked for a tour of duty in homicide before moving up to the supreme court trial bureau. They generally were rotated in one at a time and then rotated out of the bureau, in order of seniority, after about nine months of "riding homicide."

I finished my time in criminal court. As expected, I was assigned to the grand jury bureau like the majority of the those who had done their time in the criminal court. Therefore, before I started my new assignment, I took a few days off.

I did not go anywhere; it was just a long weekend to relax before starting the new position. While on my mini-vacation, I received a call on the Friday morning before the Monday I was scheduled to start in the grand jury bureau. It was the head of the criminal court bureau, who said he needed to discuss my new assignment with me.

"Steve, there has been a change of plan, you are to report to the homicide bureau on Monday."

I had a short assignment in the Homicide Bureau as I rotated through the office awaiting admission to the bar. I was aware of what the assignment to that bureau entailed. I had actually hated the couple of months I had spent there following one of the eight riding assistants around.

I did not view this assignment as practicing law, especially after having had the opportunity to try a couple of jury trials in the criminal court. Assignment to the homicide bureau, to me, was more like being a junior police officer. Yet, we lacked the authority of the police, while having at least some of the danger of going to the worst areas of the county, in the middle of the night.

The chief of the criminal court was telling me I would now become one of the eight assistants assigned to "riding" homicides who were on an eight-day rotation. When it was your turn up on rotation, you were on call from 6 a.m. until 6 a.m. the following day. Any crime that resulted in a death or a serious injury; that might result in death, required the "riding" assistant to go out to the scene of the crime, if the body was still there.

In instances when the person who died had survived long enough to be transported to a hospital, you went to the police homicide district covering the location of the crime. If there was still a body at the scene of the crime, the body could not be removed until the riding assistant had arrived.

If there were witnesses to the crime, a court stenographer would meet you and either at the scene, or at the police station, you would take witness statements. Occasionally, if there were other witnesses who had been wounded but were strong enough to provide a statement, the riding assistant and stenographer would go to a local hospital to take the statement.

If there was a suspect you would give the suspect the required "Miranda warnings" advising of their right to remain silent and the right to an attorney before speaking to anyone. If the suspect was willing to talk, after you provided the required warnings, you would take a statement which was taken down by the stenographer who accompanied you.

If the suspect was in custody but had not been identified yet by any of the witnesses, you might conduct a lineup to ensure the correct person was in custody. To preserve the evidence, you would take a picture of the lineup, using a black and white polaroid instant camera, to use as evidence, in case the fairness of the lineup was later questioned. Further, the police could not make a formal arrest for murder unless authorized by the riding assistant on duty.

As part of that job, the assistants also investigated complaints against the police and worked on helping with the investigations into unsolved homicides.

On the days you were on call you also answered legal questions posed by police officers, who called in to the office. The police officers always asked your name so they could make a notation in whatever report they filed that they had acted on the advice of a particular assistant DA. Therefore, it was important that you wrote a report about every call, in case there was later a question concerning what you had advised the police officer to do in each instance.

The riding assistants were all a year or two out of law school. With a rare exception we were in our mid-twenties. The detectives who handled homicide investigations were generally men (only men then) who, for the most part, had been in the department for twenty years or more. They hated having to wait for permission to make arrests or take other actions at the direction of these young "kids." While I did not know it would be something that could happen when I was initially assigned to homicide, on more than one occasion, while in the bureau, a frustrated detective would try to intimidate me.

In addition, it was not that many years after the United States Supreme Court had come down with several rulings protecting the rights of individuals accused of crimes. These required police and prosecutors to take certain actions, like Miranda warnings, or other rules concerning treatment of suspects, to protect the rights of the defendants.

Some of these veteran detectives did not like having to follow all these new rules and sometimes pushed back against our insistence on following them. As a result, while we worked closely with the police, there was a fair amount of tension between us and some (not all) of the detectives who felt these youngsters were interfering with their ability to conduct their investigations.

Often the murder suspects were still roaming the neighborhoods where we went to look at dead bodies, some of which had been horribly mutilated. Our duty was to ensure that legal procedures were followed by everyone involved in the investigations, keep our wits about us, while deprived of sleep 20 or more hours into a shift as we questioned witnesses and sometimes the suspects regarding specifics of these awful crimes.

During my call with the criminal court bureau chief advising of my new assignment, I objected to the changed assignment from grand jury to homicide. I thought about the time I had spent in homicide as part of my rotation through departments before I was admitted to practice law and how I hated every minute of it.

Looking at dead bodies that were shot, cut up or otherwise mutilated was not what I had signed up for. My opinion then was that the Homicide Bureau chief and the overall working conditions were unpleasant. I really did not want to go back to that bureau and play junior cop while running all over the county in the middle of the night. I wanted to practice law and moving to the grand jury bureau at least made me feel more like being a lawyer and in my mind put me closer to my goal.

Moreover, looking toward the future, what would impress a future legal employer about my work in the homicide bureau? After several months in the criminal court conducting hearings and trials, I felt this assignment was going backwards.

I was advised by the chief of the criminal court bureau that George, the head of the homicide bureau, because the bureau was high profile, had his pick of riding assistants. George had indicated he wanted me.

In the administration of the office this was viewed as a plum assignment giving the assistants assigned to the bureau a great deal of independence to take actions without close supervision. Because assistants were largely on their own during the rotation as riding assistants, George wanted people who had shown initiative to be in those positions.

"I really do not want to go back to homicide. I spent time there and hated it. I have been trying cases for months, now I will have to go play junior police officer. Is there any way I can avoid this assignment?"

"Steve, George has his pick of assistants and because of his department being the highest profile department in the office, he has a lot of power. If you turn this assignment down your career in this office is effectively done. They will bury you somewhere, like the complaint room, that will not get you into a courtroom, ever. Turning down this assignment would be a very poor move on your part."

I thought for a few seconds and agreed to the change. Clearly, I really did not have much of a choice. Being sent back to somewhere like the complaint room would be much worse. Next stop: the homicide bureau.

8

CHAPTER 8
THE HOMICIDE BUREAU

The bureau, in addition to the Chief, George and the Deputy Chief Barry, included several detective investigators who assisted the eight "riding" assistant DAs. If you were one of the eight, you were given the day off following your day in the rotation riding homicide, although you had to have all your handwritten reports into the office for typing before 9 a.m. of the day following your rotation. There was no such thing as a desktop computer or email. As a result, everything we did was handwritten and had to be turned over to a typist.

Because the cases we handled sometimes hit the news, George had to be prepared to deal with the press inquiries concerning the various shootings and stabbings that regularly occurred on our shifts. George wanted to be able to answer questions about what was going on when contacted by the news services the morning after a homicide. Without our reports there was often no way for him to know what had happened the night before.

Often our handwritten reports contained unpleasant language. Many of the assaults and murders resulted from arguments involving the exchange of a significant amount of cursing by the perpetrator of the crime and/or the victim of the homicide. As we tried to be accurate in our reports and provide context regarding what had occurred, we included the details of those arguments. Yet, one of the typists who prepared our reports refused to "type those disgusting words".

As a result, we would often get the typewritten reports back with blanks where the curse words had been written. When we complained that the reports made no sense with all the blanks, we were advised the typist was civil service and there was nothing that could be done to force her to fill in the blanks. It seemed we worked in two different worlds. The world we lived in while riding homicide with police, dead people and the witnesses to these horrible crimes and the world in the office with government bureaucracy and civil service rules.

On the weekdays, between rotations, we worked on following up investigations of the cases we "caught" during rotation, or old unsolved cases, the so called "cold cases." In addition, on weekdays we prepared witnesses and presented cases to the grand jury to seek indictments where arrests had been made on cases we caught on rotation or the occasional cold case that was solved. Part of our job was also to answer legal inquiries from the police and to investigate certain complaints against the police.

As I previously pointed out, the year I was assigned to the Bureau there were approximately 400 killings in Brooklyn alone. As we were required to respond, when on rotation, to any homicide, some unexplained deaths or any serious assault, that might result in death, we were generally busy on the days we had rotation.

Weekends were particularly difficult, often requiring whoever was covering to be out on call for 26 to 28 hours. Murderers did not follow a 9 to 5 schedule. Once you were called out on an investigation, you had to stay until all the witnesses and any suspect had been interviewed. Therefore, if you were on call from 6 a.m. Friday until 6 a.m. on Saturday and a call came in at 4 a.m. on Saturday, it was likely you would be working that case well beyond 6 a.m. on Saturday. If you were unlucky enough to have a new case come in at the beginning of your shift at 6 a.m. on Friday and then catch another early Saturday morning, along with a few in between, you could have a very long day out on calls.

There was always a "second man" assigned to help cover, if it got too busy, but we had an unwritten understanding among the riding assistants to not call out the second man unless it was absolutely necessary. I only broke that unwritten rule once.

While occasionally, a woman who was a criminal law investigator, waiting to be admitted to the Bar, would be assigned to the Homicide Bureau for a short time, no women were assigned to the Bureau as riding assistants. Apparently, although unspoken, it was felt in those days to be inappropriate to send women to the gory scenes we visited in bad neighborhoods, late at night.

On one occasion, during a daytime homicide, I had a woman criminal law investigator assigned to me at the scene of a homicide. A detective asked if he should give some information I had requested, to my "secretary." I had to explain that she was not my secretary but a law school graduate awaiting bar admission and he could give me the information. He appeared shocked that this young woman was about to become an assistant DA. What he did not know was that two of the toughest and smartest assistants I had the opportunity to work with during my time as an assistant DA were women.

I reported for work at the Homicide Bureau on Monday following my call with the chief of the criminal court bureau. I reported to George, the head of homicide, who called in the assistant I was going to replace, For my first week assigned to the Bureau I was told to follow the assistant, Jeff, whose place I was to take, so that I could become familiar with all the office procedures, as well as the cold case files I would be taking over from him.

We started out the first day heading to the Brooklyn House of Detention, the local jail, to hold a line up. One of the prisoners was a suspect in a murder and we wanted to see if there could be an identification. Unfortunately, the prisoners had gotten together and refused to participate in any activity that might identify one of their own in any additional criminal activity. Therefore, we never got to hold a lineup and the visit to the jail was a total waste of time. We later learned that another assistant had also tried to hold a lineup a day earlier. In that instance the prisoners did stand in the lineup, but they all pulled their shirts over their heads, making it impossible to identify anyone.

In the afternoon, I watched a case being presented to the grand jury involving a murder, which occurred during the course of a robbery. In this instance, two men broke into an apartment, tied and gagged the resident and burglarized the place. Unfortunately, the poor person who was bound and gagged died of asphyxiation from the gag. Between a confession and identification of the proceeds of the burglary in the Defendants' homes, it was a pretty strong case, resulting in the grand jury voting an indictment.

The following day I had my first day of "riding" homicide under the supervision of Jeff. Between running out on the calls for assaults and homicides and multiple inquiries from the police we had about 30 calls that day. I began to think I might get comfortable with this after watching Jeff take statements and confessions or doing them myself, with Jeff watching.

In one case, about a month earlier, a guy had gotten into an argument with his roommate and killed the roommate with a knife. Apparently, the roommate had no close friends or relatives, as no one had reported him missing. The suspect had wrapped the roommate's body in aluminum foil. Next, he varnished the package containing the body and stuck it under the bed.

It was not clear what he ultimately intended to do with the body. Storing a dead body under your bed would not appear to be a long-term solution to disposing of the body of the person you had murdered. But, then again, stabbing your roommate with a knife was not exactly a carefully thought-out solution to whatever the dispute had been.

However, the problem of how to dispose of the body more or less solved itself. After about a month, even with the careful attempt at mumification, the decaying body began to stink. As a result, the murderer became discouraged and turned himself in to the police.

One of the things I had learned early on in my career as a prosecutor was that many criminals are not too bright, and their stupidity made it easier to solve crimes. I often wondered what it would be like if they were smarter than most of them appeared to be. In criminal court, if we had to drop charges against someone for lack of evidence, we would say, "we will get him next time." More often than not there would soon be a next time in which the evidence was stronger and we were able to obtain a conviction.

A couple of days after my first day of riding the Bureau Chief, George, decided I should spend the day in his office going over the files I was taking on. Apparently, he thought I could not read them on my own and needed his expert guidance before I took on the work. Yet, during our meeting, there was not actually much time spent going over my files, even though our meeting turned out to take up most of what became a rather long day. It seemed George was everywhere at once and involved in everything that was going on in the bureau, at his home and elsewhere. In fact, he was into the details of everything that was going on everywhere, except the details of going over the files I was taking over from Jeff.

George was a large man in his fifties, with a booming voice and a consistently angry tone. He had this huge desktop microphone sitting in the middle of his desk that looked like something from a radio show in the 1940s. The microphone was connected to speakers in the hallway outside the individual staff offices in the section of the building that made up the homicide bureau.

When George wanted to speak with someone, he would press a button on the microphone. Then in his booming voice, that could probably be heard without the speakers, he would shout the name of a staff member and say "to my room immediately." I could never figure out why it was his "room" rather than his office, but I never once heard him say to my office immediately, it was always "to my room immediately."

To clarify just how loud and deep his voice was, approximately twenty years after I had left the DA's office I was having dinner in a restaurant in Manhattan. Suddenly, I heard an unmistakable voice that sent a chill down my spine. I looked across the room and there, three tables from us, was George having a conversation with someone. I had not seen nor spoken with him in all that time, but immediately recognized his voice from approximately ten feet away.

While supposedly speaking with me the day we were allegedly reviewing the files I was taking over, George displayed his full interest in and command of everything that was going on in the bureau, all the time.

While I sat in his office, he made literally dozens of phone calls. Between phone calls, he continually shouted over the microphone, sometimes in the middle of a sentence with me, for various members of the staff to come to his room. He spoke with anyone who happened to come by and stuck their head into his office. He yelled at the typists and the detective investigators assigned to the bureau.

He also personally supervised the placement of a lock on a door, because he apparently did not trust the locksmith to do it correctly. When he finished with the installation of the door lock, he screamed at the secretaries, because someone had broken the copy machine, and he was unable to make copies of something totally unrelated to the files he was supposedly reviewing with me.

In addition, while I was sitting there, he called a police inspector, his own wife and his daughter's teacher. Just when I thought he was going to begin to focus on some of the files, he took off two and a half hours (I was relieved) to go to a police department luncheon. During his "review" very few of my cases were actually reviewed but I received a full preview of what I would have to deal with over the course of my assignment to the bureau. In addition to the pressure of dealing with dead bodies, murderers, annoyed detectives and the friends and relatives of people who had just been murdered, I would have the pleasure of dealing with George's daily and sometimes hourly tirades over subjects both large and small.

The next day I learned about informants and how to protect their identities. There was an unmarked file cabinet with information on each assistant's informers that was kept locked and only George had access to it. In order to look at your informer's file, you had to ask George who would retrieve it from the locked file. This was important to ensure the safety and confidentiality of the informers.

I was then assigned to meet with one of Jeff's informers, who claimed to have information on two murders. He had overheard some conversations involving hits on two low level mobsters and provided some leads regarding the perpetrators.

While I was in the bureau one of the riding assistants had an informant who was in prison and was providing information regarding certain organized crime activities. Periodically, he would be brought down from an upstate prison to provide information to the assistant who acted as his contact.

In each instance the informant was brought in, he would let his wife know that he was coming in on such and such a date to meet with the DA. She would then arrange to prepare his favorite Italian dishes that he missed while in prison.

Apparently, so as not to create an issue as to why he was being allowed to have this food, his wife would prepare a lavish spread of delicious Italian food for everyone in the homicide bureau. We all looked forward to the informant coming in as she would arrange generous platters of pasta, eggplant and other dishes in the hallway of our wing of the office and we would all help ourselves to one of the best meals we ever had.

Of course, these informants, in addition to providing us with great food, often provided important information regarding crimes, impending crimes or unsolved crimes which led to the arrest of some very nasty people, who might otherwise never have been caught.

9

CHAPTER 9
RIDING HOMICIDE

"Riding homicide" had its own unique aspects that were, in many ways, also unique to the times we lived in the early 1970s and to those involved in the investigation and prosecution of homicides. When I was "on call" once every eight days, I had a beeper I wore on my belt or kept on my nightstand, when occasionally I had an opportunity to sleep for at least a portion of the night, that alerted me to call into the office.

There were police officers assigned to the DA's office twenty-four hours a day. One of their jobs, besides providing security and handling other matters related to the activities of the office, was to take the calls that required our attention. The beeper each of us carried was a very rudimentary device which merely buzzed when the officer on duty wanted to alert me that a call had come into the office that required my attention. It could not be used for any sort of response. As cell phones had not been invented. I had to locate a landline to call the office in response to the signal I received from the beeper.

If, because of the information I received, it was necessary for me to go out to a police station or the scene of a homicide, there were different procedures depending on where I was located at the time I received the alert that there was a matter requiring my attention.

If I was in the office, or already out on a call, I would get a patrol car to drive me where I had to go. If I happened to be home, between calls on the weekend or after regular working hours during the week, I had a special police department number to call. For security purposes and to assure that the person calling was not looking to ambush police officers I was given a code word, that changed every day. I had to give the code word when I called the phone number to have a patrol car pick me up at home and take me to the appropriate precinct or the scene of a murder.

At night, when I was already on a call, there was a civilian driver, Tony, who worked nights for the office. He would meet me at a precinct and drive me to the various calls we had and eventually drop me off at home.

However, the eight of us who were on the rotation tried to avoid calling Tony as much as possible. It was not that we had a problem with him driving us. We knew he had a day job, and we had an informal agreement among the riding assistants to let Tony sleep on a couch in the office, when we could.

Periodically, George figured out that we had not been calling Tony to drive us during a busy night. We were then lectured about using Tony, rather than calling out the police, who had other things to do. George would then follow up for a period of time, checking to be certain we were really using Tony for calls at night. Of course, once George stopped checking we would again, as much as we possibly could, avoid calling Tony out. At least until the next time George caught us trying to avoid calling Tony.

As I lived in a relatively safe neighborhood, when I had a patrol car from the local precinct pick me up, the local police officers sometimes did not seem very happy about driving me into some of the toughest neighborhoods in Brooklyn. Of course, I was not thrilled about it either but that was my job. Plus, unlike them, I was not carrying a gun.

Usually, after calling for a car, I would wait outside in front of my apartment building. Within five to ten minutes a patrol car would pull up to take me to the location of the call and drop me off. After I had identified myself to the officers I would climb into the back seat of the patrol car.

One night I called for a patrol car and went in front of the building to wait to be picked up. After waiting a lot longer than I thought it should have taken, a patrol car with two officers pulled up. They were both in the front seat licking ice cream cones. Apparently, they thought they were expected to be out on this call with an assistant DA for some time and no one would notice they had stopped on the way for a snack.

When they pulled up in front of my apartment building, I identified myself. I got into the back of the patrol car and closed the door. I was annoyed at the long wait, particularly since people were waiting for me at the scene of a homicide. Here I was staring at the two police officers who were sitting in the front seat like two little kids with their ice cream cones. I could not resist commenting on the present situation.

"Since you made me wait you could have at least asked what flavor I wanted."

"Mr. DA if you want, we can go back and get you a cone"

"No, just take me to the seven-seven."

No one in the police department said the precinct number as the seventy seventh precinct and to show we were into the lingo we would do the same and state the seven-seven or six-one, etc. I could see from their expressions they were not happy.

The 77th Precinct was in one of the worst neighborhoods in the county, or for that matter the country. In addition, the 77th precinct was one of those areas where certain groups of largely African American gangs had taken to shooting at police cars. In fact, when I rode in the back of a patrol car, I would slide down in the back seat so that my head was below the windows, just in case someone decided to take a shot at us.

We drove along in silence to the 77th precinct which was about a twenty-minute drive from my apartment. Then, to apparently demonstrate their desire to leave as quickly as possible, when we reached the street in front of the precinct house the car did not come to a full stop. The car slowed to a crawl as they told me to get out of the car. As soon as I closed the door, they made a U-turn and took off with tires screeching, leaving me alone on the street, outside the precinct.

On another night, I was called out at about 3 a.m. to a homicide in a public housing complex in Williamsburg. Today Williamsburg is one of the attractive places for young people to live, with new apartment buildings going up. Back then it was a high crime area, with a lot of teenage gangs. It was not a place a young, unarmed, white guy in a suit wanted to be at 3 a.m. in those days.

I was dropped off outside a large public housing apartment complex. I had to walk through a dimly lit, deserted courtyard by myself until I reached the lobby door. Not unexpectedly the door was locked. As there was a homicide in the building, I had expected at least one police officer stationed outside the building, particularly as the police were waiting for me to arrive. There were no police outside the building, or in the locked lobby. I had no way of reaching the police officers in the building. I also had no way of getting in. Standing outside in the dimly lit front of the building I contemplated my next move.

Suddenly, through the glass door, I saw a group of rowdy teenage boys running through the lobby jumping on furniture and wrestling with each other. Not knowing what else to do, I took out my badge, which resembled a detective's badge and tapped it on the glass door to the lobby, trying to get their attention.

As I did this, the thought occurred to me that calling attention to a group of teenagers hanging out in the lobby of public housing at 3 in the morning might not be the best idea for a guy in a suit, carrying a briefcase. But I hoped that showing them the badge would make them think I was a police detective. In addition, I really had no other choice. This seemed to be my only way to get into the building so that I could get to the apartment where the detective had indicated I could find the scene of the murder.

At first, the group of teenagers, apparently because they were making so much noise, did not hear me tapping on the glass door. Then they saw me and a couple of them came to the door, I flashed my badge again, hoping it would have the intended result. They suddenly looked serious, apparently, as I had hoped, thinking they were dealing with a police detective. They let me in without incident and I breathed a sigh of relief. Since I had been told the apartment number, I found the elevator and went upstairs. There was a uniformed police officer at the entrance to the apartment. I identified myself and he let me in.

As soon as I went in, all I saw was blood, everywhere. The walls were literally sprayed with blood from what appeared to be an arterial wound. Every few feet there were bloody handprints on the walls and there was a trail of blood on the floor. I followed the trail of blood, careful not to step in it and found the detective in charge.

He was kneeling over the dead body of a man, lying face up, who looked to be in his forties, although it was hard to tell as his most distinguishing feature was being covered in blood. The poor man had his eyes open and the only thing the detective said was, "I wish he would stop staring at me." Not a particularly helpful analysis of the situation.

It appeared the man had been stabbed at the door to the apartment and had stumbled, spraying arterial blood and holding onto the walls with his bloody hands along the way until he collapsed. There were no witnesses, no one had heard anything and there was nothing else to see. I authorized the release of the body to the medical examiner's office. Having done all I could do at the scene of the murder, a true waste of time, at three in the morning, I arranged for a patrol car to take me home.

On yet another occasion, I was dropped off about a block from the scene of a murder. The street was blocked off and the patrol car I was in could not get through. Therefore, there was no alternative to dropping me off and letting me find my way to the murder scene.

Again, it was the middle of the night on a dimly lit street. I had to walk through groups of teenagers hanging out long after they should have been home sleeping or doing homework. To make things more concerning, the homicide suspect had not be apprehended. I had no idea if he was in the crowd, whether he was armed or whether he was finished with his murderous activities for the night. Yet, there I was working my way through the crowd. Walking through the groups of people in a suit and carrying a briefcase in the middle of the night made me stand out, just a little, from the people gathered around trying to see what was going on at the scene of the murder.

At one of our periodic staff meetings one of the eight riding assistants said: "George we are the only people on the street without guns. I go to the scene of a murder, in the middle of the night, often with just our unarmed civilian driver, I get dropped off on the street. I am the only person in a suit and carrying a briefcase, so I stick out like a sore thumb. Many times, the murderer is still roaming the neighborhood and there are people hanging out, some of whom also have guns. The police have guns, why can't we be issued guns so we can protect ourselves if we are attacked on the street? When we are out on these calls we are often alone and have no form of protection."

George screwed his face into an angry expression and in his usual booming voice said: "all I need is one of you idiots running around the street with a gun, shooting at people. Then I will have to explain why you had a gun and why you were shooting at people in the middle of the night. No, you may not have guns under any circumstances and do not ask me again."

10

CHAPTER 10
SATURDAY MORNING

I was scheduled to begin my rotation at 6 a.m. one Saturday morning. Weekends tended to always be busy. With people out drinking and partying on Friday and Saturday nights and teenagers off from school, there was more than ample opportunity for people to get into fights over cigarettes, arguments over noise from rowdy people on the street, and drunken arguments, in addition to all the other mayhem people could come up with.

Plus, when there were large groups of people at clubs, bars and parties there tended to be arguments among the people present, whether they were there together or with another group. Often someone took offense at the way someone from another group looked at them or bumped into them.

This Saturday morning, when the beeper went off waking me from a deep sleep at 5 a.m., instead of the usual 6 a.m., or later, to start my shift, I knew it was going to be a bad day. It was never a good sign if I was already being buzzed before my 6 a.m. shift was even scheduled to begin.

I reached over to my nightstand and turned off the beeper. Then I slowly dragged myself out of bed, as quietly as possible, trying not to wake my wife. I went into the kitchen to use the wall phone and called the office.

The police officer at the desk in the DA's office answered the phone.

"This is Silverberg. My beeper just went off, did you buzz me?'

"Yes, we have several incidents for you to cover."

"Several already, what have you got?"

"There was a vehicular homicide where a drunk driver killed a pedestrian, a shooting at a social club with two dead and two in Kings County Hospital with gunshot wounds, I don't know their status. There was also a robbery that resulted in a homicide and a cop has been shot in a separate incident."

"What about Fred who was riding last night?"

"He has been out all night on other calls and is backed up taking witness statements on another homicide he picked up around four this morning. He probably will not be finished for at least a couple more hours. As a result, even though it is not quite your time to come on yet, we need you to pick up these cases."

I took down the details of the four incidents I already had to cover, including how to reach the detectives in charge of each incident, where they were located and hung up. I stood there somewhat stunned by the early start to my day and the number of incidents I already had to deal with. This was going to be a major problem. The office always gave priority to any police incident. The shooting of a police officer needed immediate attention and would likely take some time by itself, before even getting to the other matters.

I had four other dead and two wounded in three other separate incidents, in addition to the wounded cop. Someone had to deal with the wounded cop which could take several hours as those incidents generally involved a lot of police brass, witnesses and news people who wanted information which we had to ascertain first. I also could not let the other three incidents languish for a good part of the day. We had two wounded witnesses in the hospital and other witnesses scattered around Brooklyn from the other incidents.

The unwritten rule was not to call out the second man. I hesitated at first, trying to think of a way to juggle the entire mess and soon decided that, under these circumstances, I had to break our unwritten understanding. There was no way I could take on the police shooting in a timely manner and deal with the four homicides in a reasonable amount of time.

Reluctantly, I called my second man Jerry at home. It was only 5:15 a.m. and I knew he would not be happy. The phone rang twice, I heard the receiver being picked up and fumbled and finally a sleepy voice answered the phone.

"Hello?"

"Jerry, this is Steve." There was a pause.

"Hold on a second Steve."

I heard him put down the phone. Then a couple of seconds later, in the background, I heard a string of curses. Clearly, Jerry knew that a call from me at 5:15 in the morning, on a day when he was second man, was not a good sign for how the rest of his Saturday schedule, irrespective of what he had planned, was going to be spent. Then a few seconds later he came back and picked up the phone. I heard him take a deep breath and he said:

"Yes, Steve."

"Jerry, we have a problem."

"Based upon the time of your call, I already figured that out."

"Jerry, I have four murders in three different incidents plus a cop who is shot, in a fourth incident. As you know, office policy requires that the cop shooting has to be addressed immediately and the four murders are going to be a day's work in itself. What do you want to do? I will let you make the choice of what you cover, the cop shooting or the other four murders."

"I'll take the cop shooting, at least I may only have to spend half of the day on that one."

"Understood, probably the best choice under the circumstances."

I gave him the information on the location where the investigation was taking place and the detective in charge of the investigation. He said he would take care of it and wished me luck with the rest of my day.

By then my wife was awake and I told her what was going on. She groaned, pulled the blanket over her head, and tried to go back to sleep.

I felt the first thing I should do was to see if I could interview the two wounded shooting victims from the club, where two others had been killed. I had been told the detective in charge was at the hospital waiting to speak with them. It made sense to try to get their statement as soon as possible. As they were witnesses, it could help us in picking up any leads on the shooter or shooters. Of course, that all depended on their condition, but it was worth trying to speak to them if I could.

As was typical in such cases, everyone else in the club had scattered after the shooting. Therefore, the only definite witnesses, at this point in the investigation, were the two shooting victims who were unable to run off. While some other witnesses would probably eventually be located by the police, it would likely take days to track them down. Meanwhile, it was important to get as much information as we could, as soon as we could so that the investigation could get started.

I called the office again, advised Jerry was taking the cop shooting and arranged for the court reporter to meet me at Kings County Hospital where the two shooting victims were being treated. The hospital was located near the Coney Island area of South Brooklyn. Then I quickly shaved, put on a suit and called for a patrol car to take me to the hospital. The patrol car picked me up about ten minutes after I called.

When I arrived at the hospital, I was met in the lobby by the detective. He was typical of the homicide detectives, being a man in his early fifties who had decades of experience and now had to deal with a twenty something assistant DA a little over a year out of school.

"What have you got detective?"

"A social club very crowded with a lot of loud music banging away. One or two guys came in and started shooting. We have two DOA and two other guys wounded. One of the wounded is in surgery right now. The doctors think he will make it. The other had only a minor wound. He is upstairs in the ward. He is lucid and you can speak with him. But I have to tell you. I don't think you will get much from him. We tried and he claims he didn't see a thing"

"Not a surprise, but I must try. I have a stenographer on the way, to record whatever I can get from him. As soon as he arrives, I can go up and try to talk to the guy. What about other witnesses who were at the club?"

"The place cleared out by the time we arrived and so far, no one has come forward. I have men working the neighborhood trying to find additional witnesses. I think it will take some time before we can get anyone to come forward. These are often gang related. People are afraid of retaliation if word gets out that they even spoke to a police officer, let alone gave out any information."

"Well, I am here, so I might as well try to see what I can get from the guy upstairs."

At that point the stenographer arrived. We went up to the ward where the wounded man was recovering. He was about twenty years old, lying in bed with his slightly elevated leg wrapped in bandages. I said hello to him and, with the detective standing next to me, I introduced myself. He seemed alert and therefore I decided to see if I could get some information from him concerning the shooting.

We arranged to have his bed rolled to a corner of the ward, where he would be some distance from other patients. I hoped that would make him more comfortable in speaking with me. I went over to him with the detective and explained that we wanted to take a statement from him, as the stenographer set up his machine and found a chair to sit on.

Once the stenographer was ready, after formally introducing myself for the stenographic record, I began the questioning of the wounded man regarding the incident:

"I understand you were at the Club on DeKalb Avenue last night. What can you tell me about what happened last night when you were shot?"

"I didn't see nothing."

"Let's back up a little. About what time was it when you were shot?"

"I don't remember."

"Who were you with?"

"Some people."

"Could you be a little more specific? Do you know any of the names of any of the people you were with?"

"No, I was just hanging with some people I didn't know, talking and listening to the music."

"Do you know the name of anyone at all who was at the club last night, either before or during the time you were shot?"

"No."

"What did you see or hear?"

"I heard a bang and my leg hurt. I fell down. There was a lot of blood. I heard a couple of more bangs. I don't know what happened and didn't see nothing."

"Well, you must have seen something. Anything you remember could be helpful."

"I was on the ground bleeding. I didn't see nothing."

"Did anyone try to help you?"

"No, they all ran away and left me on the ground."

"Was there anyone you recognized from the neighborhood?"

"Just my friend Lou, who I heard is in surgery now."

"No one else?"

"Nope."

"So you are telling me you were in a local club, and you did not recognize a single person, other than your friend, who was also shot?"

"That's right man."

Clearly, he felt there was no problem acknowledging he knew the other fellow who he also knew was wounded but not anyone else. After a few more attempts to elicit any detail from him, it was clear he either was afraid to say anything, or really did not see anything. Although, most likely the former. Either way, it was clear he was not giving us anything useful and therefore, we were not getting any information from him.

I spoke to the detective. There were no leads on the shooter(s). He reiterated there was no one else to speak with, since the place had mostly cleared out right after the shooting. While there were a few people remaining they all claimed to have not seen or heard anything, other than some bangs. The other wounded man would be in surgery for several more hours. As a result, there was no use waiting around at the hospital and no one else worth questioning.

I asked the detective to call the office and ask for me if he got any more information that would help in the investigation. I would just have to open a new file on the matter and see what developed over the next few days. Meanwhile, I had the two other murders to investigate left over from Friday night before my regular Saturday murders started piling up. It was time to move on to my next murder investigation.

My next stop was at a homicide district that included two precincts where the other two homicides had occurred before dawn.

For the vehicular homicide, a drunk man plowed into a woman crossing the street. She was rushed to the hospital where she died. The driver of the car that struck her was too drunk to speak with. In addition, after hitting the woman he had run his car into a telephone pole causing him injuries that put him in the hospital. Therefore, the dead woman and the driver had been removed and there was no one for me to see at the scene.

At the precinct, I spoke with the only witness who provided the basic details. There was not much else to do on that case and the physical evidence was adequate without a lot of statements. There was no need for a large investigation by our office or the police. We would put the case in the grand jury early the following week and seek an indictment against the driver for manslaughter, assuming he survived and could be prosecuted.

As I was finishing up a few notes about that interview with the sole witness to the vehicular homicide, the Detective who was handling the felony murder involving the robbery came in. Again, it was the typical career police officer in his fifties with a bit of a paunch, who came bursting into the interview room. He took a stance with his feet apart and placed his hand on the gun on his waist, giving the clear impression he was getting ready to use it, if he didn't hear what he wanted to hear.

"I have been waiting for hours for you to show up, I have two witnesses out there who are getting tired. You better take them now!"

"Relax detective. I have four homicides I must deal with this morning. I was called out at 5 a.m., an hour before my shift was to start, because the assistant covering last night is backed up with other homicides. I know it is frustrating to wait and you have probably been on duty all night and would like to go home. Please give me one minute to finish my notes on the last witness I interviewed from my third homicide of the day. Once I finish my notes, then you can bring in your witnesses."

There was a grunt, then he turned and angrily marched out of the room.

I finished my notes on the third homicide. Then I brought his witnesses in, one at a time. It was a typical case. A guy tried to rob someone with a gun, the victim did not respond quickly enough to suit the robber and was shot. The gunman, who the witnesses claimed not to know, ran away. They gave a description of the shooter and that was about all we could get from them. This matter would be another new file for my follow-up in the weeks to come.

Somehow it was now mid-afternoon, I had been out since shortly after 5 a.m. I had not even had a cup of coffee. Besides already being exhausted and knowing I still had to be on call until six the next morning, I was getting hungry. I had no other calls yet and thought I would get someone to take me home. I could have something to eat and maybe sneak in a quick nap before the Saturday evening festivities started.

As I got up to leave, my beeper went off. I called into the office. The police officer covering the office, who was not the same as the one who had called me at 5 a.m. and had already gone home for the day, advised me there was another homicide and they needed me to report to another precinct to take statements from the witnesses.

The stenographer and I went to the desk officer in the precinct and got a patrol car to take us to the other precinct.

On arrival, I met with the detectives in charge of the case. "We have a shooting of a young male. He was transported to Kings County Hospital where he expired. There are two witnesses here for you to take statements."

"What about the shooter?"

"We have description of a white male, in his early twenties, curly blonde hair and chubby. Apparently, he is known in the neighborhood. We have a lead as to his whereabouts and we have a couple of teams of men out looking for him."

"OK, keep me posted on any progress finding the guy."

They brought in the first witness for me to question. I basically got into introducing myself and explaining what we were doing when I saw two uniformed cops with a chubby blonde young man walk by the window of the room I was in. I stopped the interview, got up, went out of the room and located the Detective Lieutenant in charge of the homicide district where the precinct was located.

"I just saw a chubby blonde guy being walked across the hall. Is that our suspect?"

"Does the captain of one team tell the captain of the other team what he is doing."

"No, but I was under the impression we are on the same team. My job is to make certain the entire team follows all of the rules. That is why I am out here in person, to be certain the rules are followed so we don't blow a prosecution on some technicality that was not followed. Is that the suspect?"

"Not yet."

"Well, if he becomes a suspect remind your guys they have to give him his Miranda warnings before questioning him and if I am still here I need to be brought in to take his statement with the court stenographer. If I have already left, I need to come back and take a formal statement from him."

"Understood."

"Please, let's not screw this up."

Of course, a twenty-six-year-old Assistant DA lecturing a veteran police detective lieutenant was not something that happened very often. Nor was it something that endeared me to the lieutenant.

I was concerned that I would hear about the incident from my boss, but my primary concern was that many of these older detectives were not happy that recent court decisions had changed the way they were permitted to operate. As a result, a few of them liked to make their own rules. I was there because I was required to be certain all the rules set up by the courts and the statutes were followed, so that a criminal did not get off on a technicality.

I was also a bit put off by his comment about captains of different teams. Clearly, they viewed the young assistant district attorneys as an annoyance and an impediment to the procedures they preferred to follow, which did not necessarily include all those new rules the courts recently imposed.

I went back to the room to finish with the witness. A few minutes later I was advised the chubby blonde guy was a suspect. I finished with the witness and had the suspect brought in.

With the stenographer taking everything down I gave the suspect his Miranda warnings. I questioned him about the homicide. Not surprisingly, he denied knowing anything about anything. Yet, there was enough information from the witnesses to make an arrest.

It was getting dark out, I had been involved in this insanity since 5 a.m. and had not had a chance to stop for anything, except to grab a quick sandwich between calls. As I was finishing with our chubby blonde suspect, I was beeped again. I called the office and the officer on the desk advised that I had another homicide in a different precinct.

Of course, I did, it was now Saturday night and the shootings and stabbings not only continued but as was typical on Saturday nights, they increased in number and intensity. My stenographer went home, as they were not on a 24-hour shift and a new stenographer was to meet me at the next precinct.

When I arrived, I was met by the detective in charge.

"What have we got detective?"

"Two 17 year old teenagers. One was smoking and the other asked for a cigarette. The smoker told him go to hell and the other guy pulled a gun and shot the smoker."

"I don't get these kids. Killing someone because they wouldn't give you a cigarette?"

"Steve, you have to understand the way they live. They see so many people they know in jail or dead by the time they are twenty, they feel they have nothing to lose by just doing whatever they feel like doing and they have no concern for the consequences."

"Any witnesses?"

"Yeah, a friend of the smoker."

"OK, let's go talk to him."

We went into the interview room. I took a statement from the witness which tracked the version of the incident the detective had given to me. I tried to take a statement from the shooter, but he was completely uncooperative. Yet again we had enough for an arrest, without having a confession from the shooter.

By the time I finished with them I had another call.

The police had picked up a guy who was wanted for shooting his friend in an argument. I was called and asked to come to the station house to advise the suspect of his Miranda rights and, if he was willing to talk, to take his confession. I arrived at the precinct. The stenographer arrived a few minutes later and set up his machine to take down the statement.

I spoke briefly with the detective in charge, who filled me in on what had happened. He said it appeared the suspect was willing to talk. The suspect, a man in his early twenties, with a slight build was brought into the room by the detective in charge, who was a veteran homicide detective in his mid-forties.

The suspect sat down across from me at the table, with the stenographer at the end of the table and the detective next to the suspect. I introduced myself and gave the suspect his "Miranda" warnings.

I immediately gathered from his body language that I was dealing with someone who had an attitude and wondered if he was really willing to talk. However, especially as the detective had said the suspect was willing to talk, I felt I should try to pursue the questioning, in the hope that something useful might come from the interview.

"Do you understand those rights of yours and that you do not have to speak to me if you don't want to?"

"Yes."

"Are you willing to speak to me?"

"Yes."

"Did you know a Caesar Ruiz?"

"Yes."

"I want to call your attention to the evening of November 4th of this year. Were you on Bushwick Avenue at about 11 p.m.?"

"Yes."

"Was Caesar Ruiz there at about that time?"

"Yes."

"Did the two of you have an argument?"

"No."

"Did something happen between the two of you?"

"No."

"Did you have a gun?"
"No."
"Did you obtain a gun from somewhere?"
"No."
"Did you shoot Caesar Ruiz?"
"No."
"Did you do anything at all to Caesar Ruiz that night?
"No."
"Did you see what happened to Caesar Ruiz?"
"No."

Having been told that the suspect had been ready to confess, I tried asking the questions several different ways to see if I could elicit some acknowledgement of his participation in the homicide. After several different attempts, I had an equal lack of success in obtaining any useful statement from him. He just persisted in denying anything other than being there that night and knowing Ceasar Ruiz. He claimed he did not see anything or anyone other than Ceasar and did not participate in any manner shape or form in the death of Ceasar.

"Alright detective, I guess we have nothing further to discuss."

The detective escorted the man out of the room and the stenographer, and I began to pack up our things.

About a minute later, the detective and suspect reentered the room with the suspect declaring "I want to confess."

I told the stenographer to stop packing up and I stepped out of the room with the detective. I was very concerned that this sudden change of heart by the suspect might be the result of something the detective said or did to him.

I asked: "did you do anything to him, promise him anything or threaten him in any way?"

"No, he just said he wanted to go back in."

"Are you certain?"

"Yes."

"I am going to ask him on the record, if you, or anyone else, did anything to him, promised him anything or threatened him in any way. I do not want anything along those lines to be a defense at trial, so tell me now, if I need to know anything else about what happened when you stepped out of the room with him."

"There is nothing else. We walked out and he suddenly turned around and said he wanted to go back and tell you what happened."

"OK, I hope that is his story now."

We went back into the room.

I had the stenographer finish setting up his machine again and then addressed the suspect.

"We completed questioning you a few minutes ago and you denied any involvement in the murder of Mr. Ruiz. You were out of the room with the detective for about a minute and returned declaring that you want to confess. While you were out of the room, did the detective, or anyone else, threaten you, promise you anything or do anything physical to you to make you come back in."

"No."

"Did you request to come back to speak with me voluntarily without anyone else forcing you or promising you anything if you came back in?"

"Yes, I asked to come back to you and no one promised or threatened anything."

"Are you about to make a statement to me of your own free will with this gentleman (pointing to the stenographer) taking down your statement?"

"Yes."

"I will remind you of your rights as stated to you earlier and remind you that you have the right to remain silent and you are not required to make any statement."

"Yes, I understand."

"What did you want to tell me?"

"Ruiz and I had gone out together that night and we had a few drinks. We got into an argument about a girl we both knew. He wanted to take her out. But I had already asked her to go out with me. I told him he could not go out with her as I was taking her out. He pushed me and told me I could not tell him who he could go out with. I pushed him back and told him she was my girl. Then he took a swing at me. I ducked and pulled my gun and I shot Ruiz, twice with the gun I had. Then I threw the gun in the sewer."

We then spent some time going over more of the details of what led up to the argument, the shooting, how it occurred and what he did after the shooting.

He was ultimately convicted of the killing, based largely upon his confession to me

Then, as I finished there was another call. As a result, I never got home at all on Saturday. Eventually, the assistant scheduled to take over on Sunday at 6 a.m. had the pleasure of picking up any new cases

However, my late night and early morning cases carried over to Sunday morning and as a result I did not return home on Sunday morning until about 11 a.m. I had managed to complete a lovely thirty-hour workday during which I visited a hospital, observed several dead bodies in various stages of decomposition, took two confessions and interviewed several witnesses.

Of course, before returning home, I also had to deliver my handwritten notes to the office before the news outlets started calling my boss and he started screaming for the reports. It was never clear to me how he saw the reports that were dropped off after Friday and Saturday shifts on the weekends.

Yet, he wanted them in the office so that they were available. However, the good thing was that, once I delivered all my handwritten notes, since the day following my tour riding homicide was a day off, I had the entire balance of the day after 11 a.m. on Sunday to rest and prepare for a full week of work starting at 9 a.m. on Monday morning.

11

CHAPTER 11
LINEUPS

Another one of our tasks was to periodically hold lineups. Most of the time they were related to the murders we were investigating, where the witness or witnesses did not know the suspect's name and could only describe the suspect. In those instances, we wanted to ensure that a fair identification was made before an arrest was made by the police.

There were also a few occasions where we were asked to hold lineups in cases involving other felonies where the suspect was thought to have committed multiple crimes and the police wanted to ensure all the rules were followed properly.

The lineups we held were not like the lineups depicted in movies and on television shows. At least on the occasions where I participated in conducting a lineup, there was no special room where the lineup was held with lines on the wall indicating the height of the participants. There were also no numbers on the wall behind the participants indicating how to identify them. If there were such special rooms somewhere in the New York City Police department, I never saw one while I was riding homicide.

I, and the other riding assistants, carried letter-size numbered cards in our briefcases. When we conducted a lineup, we would distribute our numbered cards and ask each participant to hold a card with a number in front of them. In addition to the suspect we would try to have other individuals in a lineup who generally bore a resemblance to the person who had been described by witnesses as the perpetrator. We tried to ensure the other participants were similar in height, weight, ethnicity, and age to our suspect. In that way the suspect did not stand out as totally different from the others in the lineup.

If the suspect was a male in his thirties and six feet tall, we tried to hold a line up with all individuals who generally met the same description. Clearly, in such a situation holding a lineup with other participants who were about five foot five and, in their fifties, would result in the person the police felt was the perpetrator standing out for the purpose of ensuring identification of that person by the witness.

Once the people in the lineup were set with their numbers, we would bring in the witness (generally separated by a one-way glass) and ask the witness if they recognized anyone in the lineup. The witnesses could clearly indicate who they identified by calling out the card number of the individual who was being identified. Then to confirm the identification was of the person who committed the crime, we would ask the witness where specifically they had seen the person before. All this would be recorded using our court stenographer to have a record of what transpired.

Generally, the police stations had polaroid cameras that took instant black and white photographs. We used those photographs to preserve a record of what the lineup looked like. In this way we could demonstrate, if necessary, during pretrial hearings that the people in the lineup were of similar age, size, and ethnicity to ensure that the lineup had been as fair as possible. We would also have the transcripts from our stenographers as the record of all conversations with the witnesses, as well as the participants in the lineup, while the viewings took place. In that way we preserved the record of what occurred in case a defendant challenged the fairness of the identification process in court.

One evening, while on my rotation, I received a request from the captain of a precinct to hold a lineup. There had been a series of muggings, over a period of several weeks in some public housing, where residents of the housing had been robbed and, in some instances, assaulted. The victims had given similar descriptions of two men involved in each of the robberies. This was long before closed circuit television cameras in the lobbies of buildings.

As a result, the only thing the police had to locate the suspects were the descriptions provided by the victims of the various muggings. The police had picked up two suspects who fit the descriptions of the men involved in the muggings provided by the victims of the muggings. As the people who had been robbed did not know the men who had robbed them it was necessary to hold lineups to see if either, or both, of the two suspects could be identified by the victims.

The precinct captain indicated to me:

"I want to have this done right. Can you come down and hold lineups? We have four victims ready to view the lineups."

"Captain I can hold the lineups, but I will need several people who look like the suspects so that the lineups are fair. If the suspect is black, we cannot have him in a lineup with just white men. We will also have to use your polaroid camera to take pictures of the lineups to preserve them for any challenge to the identification. I assume you do have a working polaroid?"

"I can have that ready for you by the time you arrive."

"Ok, captain I will see you in about an hour."

I arranged for transportation to the precinct. Upon my arrival, I asked for the captain and was brought to his office.

"Captain where are the men who will be participating in the lineup with the suspects?"

"We were not able to get anyone to volunteer off the street at this time of the night. However, I have several officers who are similar in appearance to the suspects. We don't have enough to hold separate lineups but the five officers I have will mix in well with the two suspects. I think if we use all five men in a single lineup with the two suspects it will be a fair identification process."

"Can I see the men you are planning on using?"

"Of course, I will have someone take you to where they are waiting."

I was taken downstairs where the police officers who were to participate were siting, having changed into their civilian shirts. I was introduced to them by the officer who brought me into the room. The only problem I noticed immediately was that all of them were still wearing their blue uniform pants. Looking at the men I realized this was not going to work.

Anyone who was the least bit observant would see that two of the men were in civilian clothing and five of the men were wearing police uniform pants. Yes, the camera would only record black and white photographs, so the blue uniform pants would not be particularly noticeable. However, the suspects could notice the uniform pants and raise an issue with their attorneys when the case appeared in court.

If there was any challenge to the fairness of the lineup this would be a major issue. Besides, my job was to be certain the lineup was fair. I needed to be certain that, if the suspects were identified, it would be because they were the men who had committed the crimes, not just some poor guys who had been incorrectly selected for prosecution through a biased process.

Looking at the five police officers I said:

"Gentlemen, you need to change out of your uniform pants and into all civilian clothing. The lineup must be a fair process and your uniform pants are a giveaway that you are police officers, to anyone who is the least bit observant."

There was a bit of grumbling, but they went back to the locker room to change their pants. I went up to speak with the Captain again. I explained what had happened and asked about the polaroid camera. The Captain sent an officer to retrieve the camera. Upon his return the officer announced that they could not locate any film for the camera. The Captain said we would have to do it without the film.

"First Captain, when I spoke with you when you asked me to come I specifically noted the need to take pictures of the lineup with your polaroid. We will need to send someone to get film for the camera. You asked me to come here so that it is done right. I am not wasting time holding a lineup without having a record we can use to dispute any challenge to the fairness of the lineup."

The Captain clearly not pleased with an annoying young upstart Assistant DA telling him what to do, reluctantly sent an officer to buy film at a local discount chain store that was still open that late in the evening. About twenty minutes later the officer arrived with the film for the camera.

Finally, we were ready to proceed. The problem was that the only place large enough to hold the lineup was in a hallway upstairs on the second floor of the precinct house. The only one-way window to protect the identity of the witnesses was in a small room, basically the size of a large closet, with the one-way window facing out into the hallway.

We had to keep the witnesses apart while conducting the lineups to avoid them influencing each other. Therefore, we had to put each witness into the room separately, so the other witness's perspective regarding the suspects was not altered by what another witness said or who a particular witness identified.

Once the witness was in the room, we had the one-way window covered with a shade. Then we had to bring the lineup participants into the hall, get the men in line holding their numbered cards and conduct the identification with that witness.

When that viewing was completed, we again wanted to protect the identity of the witnesses until they had to be disclosed later in the criminal prosecution. As a result, we had to move the participants in the lineup out of the hallway. This way we eliminated the ability of the next witness to observe the men before we held the formal viewing and to avoid the suspects seeing or hearing the witnesses as we moved the witnesses in and out of the viewing room.

Then we had to bring the witness out of the room and place the witness in isolation so as not to influence the next witness. Once that witness was isolated from the others, we had to move the next witness into the room and go through the whole process of bringing the participants into the hall again, lining them up, etc.

I felt like a choreographer moving the witnesses and the men in the lineups in and out of the hallway and the room with the one-way window. In addition, a process that should have taken less than an hour now took nearly two hours due to all the movement in and out of the hallway and viewing room.

Again, in my quest to try to ensure fairness and to make it harder to challenge the fairness of the lineup when the case came before a judge, I also wanted a certain degree of participation by the suspects. As a result, before each witness viewed the lineup, I followed a routine with the participants, by addressing each of the suspects. To preserve a record of what went on, I had the stenographer recording everything that was said.

With each lineup I addressed the suspects, outside of the hearing of the witness:

"We are about to hold a line up for a certain witness to view. The men who are standing here will be in the lineup. Do either of you have any objection to any of the men participating in the lineup with you?"

"No. No."

"You can each decide where in the lineup you want to stand."

The two suspects then proceeded to look each of the officers up and down. Then they had the officers move around to change the order in which they were each standing.

Then I continued:

"You have now had an opportunity to choose the order in which you are standing. Are you both satisfied with everyone's position in the lineup?"

"Yes. Yes."

We took a photograph of the lineup. The stenographer and I then went into the room where a single witness was waiting. We pulled up the shade covering the one-way window. With each witness I would then address him or her with the stenographer taking down anything that was said to or by the witness.

"On July 8th of this year, you reported that two men mugged you in the elevator of your apartment building, stealing your watch and wallet. Please look at the men in the hallway holding numbers and see if any of these men look familiar to you."

If either or both suspects were identified, I asked the witness to explain where they had been seen, to clarify that he or they were the robbers and not just someone they had seen on the street in the neighborhood.

After each witness we conducted our choreography of moving everyone around. I would again do the same routine with the suspects, asking if they were satisfied with the order in which everyone was standing. One of the suspects, for some reason I will never fully understand, seemed either amused by the process and thought it was some sort of a game, or perhaps he felt that if he took a different number each time he would ensure that, if a witness shared his prior number with other witnesses, the next witnesses would identify the wrong person.

Each time I brought the men back into the hallway and asked about the order of the lineup that suspect would move everyone around He would walk up and down studying each of the men in the lineup and the order in which they were standing, He would then make additional changes in where they were standing, sometimes more than once before taking a different number for himself.

He did this for each viewing of the lineup. While I suspect the officers were getting frustrated with having this suspected criminal moving them around like chess pieces, they all behaved themselves and went along with the little game the suspect was playing.

Once the two suspects acknowledged they were finally satisfied with the lineup and the order in which everyone stood, I noted for the record the numbers they were holding. With every lineup we took another photograph of the new lineup, being certain that our records showed which lineup was viewed by each witness and the photograph that coincided with that specific lineup.

It was tedious to say the least. Yet, it had to be fair both to be certain we had fair identifications and that any identifications would stand up to scrutiny by the courts. If either or both suspects were identified, the identifications had to be accurate. The identification process had to be as protected from a successful challenge as was reasonably possible.

At the end of the long process, each of the defendants had been identified more than once and none of the police officers, who did resemble the suspects in ethnicity, age, height and weight, had been selected by any of the witnesses. As a result, I had a fairly high level of confidence as to the fairness and accuracy of the process we conducted in holding the lineups.

The witnesses were thanked for their participation and told they could return home. As we were wrapping up, one of the witnesses, a slight woman in her fifties, came back to ask a question.

Unfortunately, she was apparently under the impression that the men in the lineup were all criminals. After all, who else would be standing in a lineup but a bunch of criminals? As she rushed back into the hallway to ask her question before we left, she came face to face with one of the police officers who had participated in the lineup. She stopped about a foot in front of him, gave a brief shout and passed out, apparently thinking she had come face to face with a dangerous criminal, who was now on the loose.

A couple of the officers carried her into an office to give her a chance to recover, while I packed up and headed home, until my next call. In retrospect, I assume her reaction in coming face to face with the police officer proved that I had done my job in conducting a fair lineup, as the witness clearly thought all the men she observed in the lineup were criminals of some sort and did not pick up on the fact that five of them were police officers.

12

CHAPTER 12
MOB "HITS"

Organized crime has a long history in New York City. During my stint in Homicide there was an ongoing gang war among several of the "Five Families" of the New York Mafia who were competing for control of various criminal activities.

This resulted in a large number of murders throughout the City of New York. During that time period Brooklyn received more than its fair share of these mob "hits." Several of the murders involved the high-level members of the various gangs. Those murders made headlines and all the local news shows. Sometimes the coverage lasted for days, with reports every morning and evening of the "latest" developments in the investigations of these crimes.

In those days, there was no twenty-four-hour news coverage. If something could not fit into the morning or evening news shows that were often between fifteen and thirty minutes in total, it was not covered. The murder of a low-level gangster was often not important enough to make the limited television news coverage of the day. While these murders would sometimes make the back pages of the local newspapers, they garnered very little public awareness. Unfortunately, the police and those of us in the District Attorney's Office still had to cover these crimes and try, with little help from anyone, to find a way to solve them.

Those of us in the homicide bureau were tasked with going to the scenes of the homicides and working with the police department in investigating those murders, often with little success. As a result of the obvious concerns people had about potential retaliation for cooperation with the police, there were rarely any people who admitted to witnessing anything related to these often-vicious murders.

In each of these investigations, canvassing neighborhoods rarely resulted in anyone acknowledging that they had seen or even heard anything unusual. This lack of knowledge appeared inconsistent with the fact that there were often nearby shootings, in the evenings, when people were in their homes or businesses, sometimes just feet away from the crimes that had been committed with multiple gunshots.

These killings tended to follow a standard pattern. They occurred at night, there were never any witnesses brave enough to admit to witnessing one of these murders or hearing anything out of the ordinary. To make it clear that the killing was a "hit" and not a robbery, any jewelry the victim had on, like expensive watches and rings, along with wallets and often, large amounts of cash were left intact.

Clearly, in each instance a message was being sent to other members of the gangs. This will be your fate should you cause any issues for anyone in my gang, or otherwise fail to adhere to the orders you receive or the rules you are instructed to follow by the "boss" of the "family".

As part of my usual rotation, I had exposure to a couple of these hits. On one occasion, I was called out to an apartment building in the Bensonhurst section of Brooklyn, a largely Italian neighborhood in those days. When I arrived, there was a rather large police presence, with several police cars and patrol officers outside the building. I was escorted by an officer to the third-floor hallway of the apartment building. There I met the detective in charge who was with two other detectives.

In the hallway, lying faceup, was a man of about fifty. He was well dressed. His most distinguishing features were the several bullet holes in his face. He was lying with a pool of blood around his head and upper torso. In fact, it appeared that the force of the bullets striking his face threw him onto his back. It also appeared the bullets striking his face had been powerful enough to cause his toupee, which was lying on the floor about six inches behind him, to fly off his head.

The detectives were waiting for the medical examiner to arrive to examine the body, although the bullet holes in the victim's face made the cause of death obvious, even to a novice like me.

As usual in these cases, the victim was wearing jewelry, consisting of the usual expensive watch and diamond pinky ring. He also had a large amount of cash in his wallet. He was at the end of the hallway. It was late in the evening and his body was close to the entrance doors of three apartments, one at his head and one on either side of where his body was lying.

The hallway was so narrow that a detective had to straddle the body, with one foot on either side of the body, to allow him to reach the apartment doors on either side of the body. The detective knocked on each door and someone opened each door, just a crack, when the detective flashed his badge in front of the peep hole.

Curiously, while there were people awake in each of the three apartments, who heard the not very loud knocking on the door, no one admitted to hearing a sound coming from the hallway. While I suppose it was possible a silencer was used, that was not generally part of the equipment used for these murders.

Those who peeked out their doors, after the detective knocked, claimed to be shocked to learn someone had been shot several times within a couple of feet of their doorway. As it was clear more than one shot was fired, the people in the apartments clearly had no interest in trying to find out what happened in the hallway when the shots were fired. Or, if they did know what happened in the hallway, they felt that playing oblivious was safer than providing any information.

The only person in the building who knew anything at all was the person who discovered the body when he returned home to the building. He had entered the hallway and seen the bloody body lying on the floor and gone into his apartment on the other end of the hall and called the police.

However, the victim was already dead and the man who discovered the body claimed to have seen nothing. Therefore, there was no purpose in my taking a formal statement from him. There was nothing he could add to the investigation and the police had whatever meager information the man provided.

As in other similar instances, the victim had known ties to organized crime. We had no idea what the victim had been doing in the apartment building. No other witnesses came forward. No one acknowledged knowing him or why he was in the building. During my time in the Bureau, little was developed in the way of additional evidence. As was the case with many of these mob murders, no one was charged with that murder during my tenure.

While I was serving in Homicide, my wife and I decided to move. We had been in a one-bedroom rent controlled apartment which was all we could afford when we first got married and I was finishing law school. We decided, since we now had a reasonable income that a move to a larger apartment in a nicer building would be a good idea. It turned out that the day we had to move I was assigned to take my turn on call for the day. No one wanted to change shifts with me. However, I was able to arrange for someone to cover for me until 5 p.m., as it was a weekday and there was rarely much activity for those of us in the Homicide Bureau to cover before the sun went down on weekdays.

Although moving is never fun, the move went as well as could be expected and the movers left our new apartment at about 4:30. Just as we were beginning to try to put the bed frame together, so that we could put the mattress on it and have a comfortable place to sleep that night, my office beeper went off.

I had a call that had just come in and, as it was now almost 5 o'clock, I was no longer entitled to dispensation of coverage that would last beyond 5 p.m. Whoever was covering for me until 5 o'clock made it clear to the officer at the desk that, since it was now 4:45, I was to be called,

I quickly changed into a suit, found my briefcase among the rubble in the new apartment and called for a patrol car to transport me to my first call of the evening. Unfortunately, I left my wife with the mattress on the floor and boxes piled up all over the apartment. To say the least, she was not thrilled being left with the mess. Unfortunately, I was on call that day and had no choice but to go back to work.

The call was relatively routine for a Homicide Bureau riding assistant. But I had to visit the scene and then interview several witnesses. As a result, I had to spend a large part of the evening in the precinct taking statements from the witnesses.

As I was finishing writing up my notes, I was hoping I could head home to my new apartment and begin unpacking, or at least put together the bed frame, so we could sleep in our bed. But just as I was about to get a ride home, I was beeped. Another call had come in about a body in a car in the Coney Island area. Instead of going home, I had to get a patrol car to bring me to the location of the body in the car and see what was happening there.

By the time I arrived at the scene of the homicide there was a steady rain. Luckily, I was wearing my standard trench coat, looking like the T.V. character, detective Columbo. There were a number of detectives and uniform officers standing around a late model Cadillac, the model of choice for many in organized crime at that time. In the car, slumped over, with his forehead resting on the steering wheel, was a well-dressed man in his forties wearing a suit and tie. The only thing unusual was that he had a couple of bullet holes in the back of his head and blood hanging from his nostrils.

Shortly after I arrived our driver, Tony, showed up to transport me when I was finished at the site. Then a photographer from a local newspaper showed up. The news photographer was trying to get a photograph of the body, I don't know why no one tried to stop him, perhaps because it was so unusual to have any news coverage, and no one knew how to handle it. The photographer was aided by Tony. Tony stood proudly with a big grin on his face, at the driver's side window of the car with the body slumped over the steering wheel, shining a flashlight on the body. Clearly Tony was hoping to get his picture in the newspaper as well. Unfortunately for him, he was edited out of the picture that appeared in the next day's paper.

Meanwhile, as this was a neighborhood of single-family residences and the car was directly in front of a couple of houses, the police began knocking on the doors of the houses to find out if anyone had seen or heard anything. As usual, no one acknowledged seeing or hearing anything out of the ordinary, until the police knocked on their door.

After the police finally chased away the photographer, they began going through the car. The deceased was wearing the usual expensive watch and a diamond pinky ring. He had almost two thousand dollars in his pocket which would be roughly about fifteen thousand dollars today, not the typical petty cash most people carried even in the era before electronic fund transfers.

As usual in these cases, he still had his wallet in his pocket as well. He also had a small notebook in his pocket with lists of names. Clearly the message to all was that this is a gang hit. As the car and trunk of the car were searched by the detectives some other documents were found scattered around and in his pockets.

Of course, while I was standing there a patrol car pulled up and another detective, who looked to be in his forties, jumped out of the back of the patrol car looking for the "DA." I identified myself. It turned out he had a question concerning how to charge someone he had in custody. As I was on call for police inquiries as the riding assistant for the day, I pulled my trusty Penal Code out of my briefcase, took his information, so that I could write a report on what we discussed, and the answer to his questions.

By that time the rain had started getting heavier. It was decided, as there were no witnesses to question, we should get out of the rain and go back to the precinct to look over the papers that were found.

Back at the detective's office they began to go through the bloodstained notebook and other documents they had found in the car and on the body. It soon became clear from the contents of the notebook and other papers that the victim was a bookie. The notebook contained a list of his clients and other documents showing the bets that were taken. Strangely, neither the name of the victim nor that of any of his customers were Italian sounding names. Everyone appeared to be of a different ethnic background.

It was now about one in the morning. We had been at this both on the street and at the precinct for several hours. There was nothing in the documents that was particularly helpful in getting to any sort of quick resolution of the murder. The lead detective, in complete frustration, swept the papers off his desk with his hand and onto the floor declaring: "what kind of mafia hit is this with not one Italian name, including the victim's?"

With no witnesses and no leads, I had done what little I could do. It was time for me to leave and try to finally get back to my new apartment with the piles of belongings that had not been unpacked and the bed that had not been put together.

As I had not had dinner, and we were in Coney Island, Tony and I decided to stop to see if the "Nathan's Famous" hot dog stand was still open. If possible, we could each get a hot dog. Before leaving the precinct I decided to call my wife, as we had not spoken since I ran out just before 5 o'clock, I wanted to at least let her know I was OK. I called the new apartment and woke her.

"Hi, I wanted to let you know I am OK, and out at a homicide in Coney Island. Since we had no dinner, I wanted to know if you want a hot dog from Nathans, as I am going to stop before I head home and try to get something?"

There was a short pause and then, in a sleepy voice, my wife said: "don't call this number again" and hung up.

13

CHAPTER 13
MEDICAL EXAMINER

A key component of the prosecution of any homicide is establishing the cause of death. Without a medically determined cause of death establishing that the death resulted from homicide, even if the cause appears obvious a defendant cannot be found guilty beyond a reasonable doubt of having caused someone's death.

The New York City Medical Examiner's Office had several highly qualified physicians, trained in performing autopsies to determine the exact cause of death of the various victims of the crimes we investigated. While the doctors were accurate 99.99 percent of the time, occasionally, like all humans subject to fatigue, overwork or other factors, they made a mistake.

Some of the mistakes would have been laughable if we were not dealing with such serious issues. Luckily, those mistakes were very few and usually could be corrected. Although, those rare errors were somewhat stunning when they did occur.

One night, when I was out on another one of the unending calls, I was beeped. When I called in to the office I was told to check in with a detective on a death. I was able to reach the detective. He then advised me that a man had been found dead. He was face down in the hallway of his apartment with no sign of a struggle.

However, the detective told me it was not necessary after all for me to come out as, immediately after calling the case into the DA's office, the Medical Examiner arrived at the scene of the death. The Medical Examiner had determined that the man in question had apparently died of a drug overdose. There was nothing suspicious about the body or anything they or the medical examiner had observed at the location where the body was found. The body would be taken to the morgue where it would be more thoroughly examined, Meanwhile, I could skip coming out to the scene.

I was delighted that I had one less stop to make late at night. I made a few notes concerning my conversation with the detective and finished up with the case I was already out covering.

About half an hour after I had spoken with the detective, I was beeped again. When I called the office, I was told I needed to call the same detective back about the body that had been found. This was highly unusual.

As a rule, once I had been advised the medical examiner had determined the death was not suspicious, and I had been advised, because of the medical examiner's determination, I was not needed that would usually be the end of the issue. If at some later date other evidence was discovered I might be called again, but at least for the initial call I was finished, based upon the medical examiner's initial determination that the death was not suspicious. Getting a call back just half an hour after being advised, based on the preliminary opinion of the medical examiner that there was nothing suspicious about the death, was unheard of. I called the detective back and had the following conversation with him:

"We need you to come to the precinct to speak with a witness."

"What witness? You told me the M.E. said the guy died of an overdose."

"Yeah, I know. Apparently, the M.E. didn't bother to turn the guy over when he examined the body in the apartment. After our call the morgue attendants came to take the body to the morgue. When they arrived, unlike the medical examiner, they did turn the body over. They immediately noticed blood on his chest. After a closer look, it appears he was shot."

"I don't understand how the ME decided it was an overdose without examining the body?"

"Steve don't ask me I am only reporting what I have been told, but now what we thought was an OD is an apparent homicide from a gunshot wound. Once we found out it was not an overdose, we made some additional inquires and we have discovered a witness."

I had no choice but to head out and take a statement from the witness.

On another occasion I was called out early one morning to a single room occupancy building where the body of a woman had been found. These buildings in poorer neighborhoods would have several bedrooms on a floor, somewhat like a shabby hotel, where people lived. Just a single bathroom on each floor was used by the occupants of all the individual bedrooms on that floor.

There were no elevators. The stairwells and the hallways were poorly lit and had a musty odor. They were bleak places, with piles of debris in the halls and swarming flies as you walked in. It was truly sad that people lived in these conditions, but I assume it was still better than living on the street.

I walked up the stairs to where a police officer was standing guard. He directed me to a room down the hall where a couple of detectives were examining the premises.

The room was small, dark, and dirty. It contained a dresser and a bed with a woman lying face up on the bed. She looked like she was probably in her late thirties. Her face had bruises in a number of places, giving the appearance of someone who had been beaten. She also had blood on the front of her nightgown. The blood looked like it had been vomited up. Between the bleak room and the poor bloodied woman lying alone face up on her bed it was all a rather sad scene of poverty and death.

I was advised by one of the detectives that the woman lived alone and apparently a neighbor had found her that morning after she failed to come out of her room. He also advised me there were no witnesses.

Not even the person who had called in stating they had found a dead body had come forward after leaving the message. It appeared that the unfortunate people who lived in these bleak conditions tried to have as little contact as possible with the police.

Looking around the small room, I noticed what appeared to be a man's smoking pipe among the clutter on the dresser.

"If she lives alone, whose pipe is that?"

"What pipe?"

I pointed: "the one on the dresser, right here."

The detective turned to where I was pointing and acknowledged they had not noticed the pipe yet.

There were no witnesses and therefore no one to speak with, so I went on to my next adventure of the day.

About two days later I received a death certificate for the woman. It stated the cause of death as natural causes. I was confused as, based upon my uneducated observations of the bruises on her face and the blood on her nightgown, she looked like someone had beaten her rather badly and she had died because of her beating. I called the Medical Examiner's Office and got the doctor who had signed the death certificate on the phone.

"Doctor, I received the death certificate today for Pamela Fitzpatrick and it states she died of natural causes. I am confused by your findings. While I do not claim to be an expert, I saw the body. It looked to me like she had been badly beaten. She had some large bruises on her face and there was dried blood on the front of her clothing. I don't understand how her death could be determined to result from natural causes."

"Yes, it was natural causes. She had a spontaneous gastric hemorrhage which caused the blood you saw on the front of her nightgown. As for the bruises, they were old and had nothing to do with the cause of death."

"Was an autopsy performed?"

"No need to conduct a full autopsy, the cause of her death was clear from a simple examination of the body."

"OK, doctor, you are the expert. Thank you for taking the time to explain your conclusions to me."

I still had doubts about the result and wondered why they had cut corners and had not performed an autopsy. But I was not the medical examiner. I wrote a memo closing my file on the matter noting there was no evidence of criminal activity related to the death. I was glad to have one less case to investigate.

About a week later, I received an amended death certificate for Ms. Fitzpatrick. It listed the cause of death as "cerebral hematoma homicide."

Now her "natural" death was stated to be caused by an injury to her brain and significantly was now listed as a homicide. Curious to say the least, to find out how the "obvious" natural causes without an autopsy had become a cerebral hematoma resulting from a homicide, I called the Medical Examiner's Office again. I was not able to reach the doctor with whom I had previously spoken. However, I was able to find out what had happened from one of the assistants in the Medical Examiner's office.

After the original death certificate was issued, someone had come in to identify the body, the usual process followed before the medical examiner released the body for burial.

In answering certain routine questions always asked of those present to identify the body, such as whether the person had any knowledge regarding the death of the deceased, the individual who showed up at the medical examiner's office had a detailed story to tell.

This person stated that a few people were in the dead woman's room the night she died. They were all having a drink when a man unexpectedly showed up. He got into an argument with Ms. Fitzpatrick. During their verbal altercation he went into the hallway and came back with a wooden board. He then struck her over the head with the piece of wood. After hitting her on the head he intimidated the others in the room with the board he had in his hands. He then exited with the board in his hand to discourage anyone from following him. The others in the room were all left standing there watching Ms. Fitzpatrick.

After being struck in the head Ms. Fitzpatrick told the people who were still in her room that she did not feel well and asked them to let her rest. Respecting her wishes, the others left her room. Apparently, no one checked on her during the night to see if she needed assistance. She was found dead the next morning. Someone anonymously called the police when the body was found but no one came forward when the police were at the scene of the death.

Based upon these new statements by the person who came to identify the body, the Medical Examiner decided that perhaps he should conduct a full autopsy. The autopsy determined that she had a cerebral hematoma (a brain bleed) that caused her death. Based upon the description of the attack on her, as being struck in the head with a board, it was determined the death resulted from an act of homicide.

A couple of days later the police picked up the guy who was alleged to have hit her over the head and he confessed. Noting that he had just gotten out of prison. When he came to visit Ms. Fitzpatrick, he became upset she was too busy with the other people to spend time with him. As a result, they got into an argument. He picked up a board that was in the hallway and came back into the room. She would not relent and tell the others to leave, so he could be with her. He lost his temper and hit her with the board. He then went out to find another lady who would spend his first night out of prison with him and satisfy his "needs".

On yet another occasion I was reviewing the transcript of a murder trial. The doctor from the medical examiner's office went into great detail about the process he followed in performing the autopsy. He went through each step he followed in the procedure and testified regarding each of his detailed findings.

On cross examination by the defendant's attorney, he went into even more detail concerning the manner of examining various organs. The only problem with the doctor's testimony was when he was asked the final question by defense counsel. "Please look at the bottom of the last page and tell me the name of the Doctor who signed the autopsy report?"

It turned out that he had not signed nor for that matter conducted the autopsy, as a different doctor in the Medical Examiner's Office had signed the autopsy. I wondered how the assistant DA who conducted the trial explained that little oversight to his bureau chief the next day. From the transcript it appeared no one other than the defense attorney had bothered to check on which of the doctors in the medical examiner's office had signed the autopsy used to prosecute the defendant.

Thankfully these mishaps were rare exceptions to the rule.

14

CHAPTER 14
THE GRAND JURY

Part of our job was to present cases to the grand jury for the purpose of obtaining indictments in the cases involving the homicides we had investigated. The grand jury was largely a formality, as rarely did a grand jury fail to vote in favor of an indictment sought by the district attorney. Unlike an actual trial, it was not necessary to prove a crime beyond a reasonable doubt to the grand jury. Beyond a reasonable doubt is the test only at the time of trial. The purpose of the grand jury is to see if there is "probable cause" to believe a crime was committed by the person being charged with the crime.

In fact, it had been stated by one New York prosecutor, around the time I was working as an assistant, that, based on the level of proof required for a grand jury, a district attorney could "indict a ham sandwich." While a bit of an exaggeration, the statement was not a significant exaggeration of the true level of proof used to obtain an indictment (at least back then).

The process took place behind closed doors, with just the members of the grand jury, the prosecutor presenting the case and a court reporter recording the proceedings. A prospective defendant could testify but would have to waive his or her rights against self-incrimination and would not have an attorney present in the room. As a result, it was very rare that a defendant elected to testify during the grand jury proceeding.

Therefore, the members of the grand jury heard one side of the story from the witnesses selected by the D.A. to present the basic evidence of the crime to the grand jury. Then the assistant D.A. "charged" the grand jury by reading the sections of the Penal Law that the Assistant DA thought were applicable to the facts of the case. After he charged the grand jury he left the room so the jurors could deliberate and vote on whether to return the indictment on each of the charges that had been read to them.

Once the grand jurors had voted on whether to indict, they hit a button which turned on a light outside the room to notify the Assistant DA that they had reached a decision on the charges. The assistant would return to the room and the jury would advise of the conclusion they had reached on whether to indict and if an indictment had been voted, the exact charges adopted by the grand jury. The indictment would later be typed up by the DA's office and presented to a State Supreme Court judge for signature, which made it official.

To demonstrate that an indictment is merely a determination of probable cause but not of guilt, we need only look at a case I subsequently handled. After my stint in the homicide bureau, I was asked to try a case where two African American men had been accused of attempting to rob a white cab driver. As a part of my preparation for trial, I contacted the cab driver and had him come into the office to be interviewed.

He was a man in his forties, a bit overweight and dressed as you would expect to see a cab driver dressed. He came into the room and sat down across from me with his right foot crossed and resting on his left knee. As I went through what had happened with him, it became clear to me that his story had holes in it. When I pressed him on details, he was either unclear or inconsistent in what he told me.

In addition, he demonstrated what poker players would call a "tell." When I pressed him on facts, he alternated between rubbing his face, looking away from me and not making eye contact or wiggling his right foot. To me these were all signs indicating a certain level of nervous reaction to what I thought were straight forward questions.

Since these were questions about the details of the incident, he was likely going to be asked about by the defense attorney, as the complaining witness I thought he should have been able to answer the questions without all the fidgeting, He appeared to me to be like a poker player who was bluffing.

Next, I interviewed the arresting officer, who it turned out had not witnessed anything related to the actual alleged crime. I asked him about the cab driver's story and whether he thought it was shaky. The officer agreed that the story appeared to have some issues, however, he stated that, as the cabbie, a mature looking man, had insisted that the two men tried to rob him, there was no choice but to make the arrest.

I began to wonder whether this all had something to do with the cabbie being white and the two accused men being black. I did not raise that with the white police officer, who appeared to answer me honestly about the arrest and what he knew or didn't know about the incident.

After interviewing the men, I was quite concerned with what I had heard and seen from my only two witnesses for the trial. Could we be prosecuting two innocent men?

Therefore, after interviewing the cabbie and arresting officer, I went to see the deputy bureau chief in charge of the supreme court trial parts. I explained my two interviews. Then I expressed my concerns over continuing the prosecution.

We had a complaining witness who had holes in his story, no supporting evidence or witness and our only witness acted very nervous when questioned about details of his story. All these weaknesses would likely become amplified during cross examination in front of a jury.

My deputy bureau chief's response was, "these two men were indicted by a grand jury, we cannot unilaterally fail to prosecute."

I replied, "we both know we can indict anyone for anything, that does not automatically make them guilty. I think there are serious issues with this case and we should consider dropping the charges."

"Go, do your job and try the case and no more of your opinions about the witnesses."

I was a bit upset with the reaction I received but my boss was clearly not pleased with my attitude, I had been ordered to proceed and I had no choice.

A few days later we began to select a jury which took a few days by itself. The day we completed selecting the jury the defense attorney and I made opening statements which took the rest of the morning. We then broke for lunch and came back at 2 p.m. to start the testimony.

I put the cabbie on the witness stand and he went through his story of the attempted robbery in detail. As it was not my place to challenge my own witness during the trial, but merely let him tell his tale, it went reasonably smoothly. Next the defense attorney began his cross examination and, not unexpectedly to me at least, the cabbie's story began to fall apart.

The defense attorney brought out facts I had never been told. The cabbie admitted the defendants had hailed him on the street and asked the cabbie to take them to the nearby hospital. He acknowledged that one of the two defendants had a wet cloth covering his eyes. He also acknowledged the defendants had told the cabbie there had been a chemical splashed into that defendant's eyes at a construction job. None of these and other details, brought out during the cross examination, had been shared with me when I questioned the cabbie about the incident. Before the cross examination of the cabbie was completed, we adjourned for the day.

I was torn by what I was witnessing. I went back to speak to my boss. I outlined in detail the testimony, the lack of consistency and the holes in his story brought out in even greater detail by the defense attorney, who clearly had more background on what had actually occurred than I had been given by the cabbie. I noted the inconsistency of the defendants asking to go to the hospital with a chemical burn of the eyes but stopping on the way to hold up the man who was transporting them. There was also a lack of any evidence of there being a weapon.

"I told you to try the case. If it is a loser, then they will be found not guilty, but it is not our job to overrule the grand jury."

"Look, I don't care if I lose this case, I should lose it. These two men have already spent a year in jail awaiting trial because they could not make bail. I am literally terrified that I might convince this jury that these two black guys tried to hold up a white cabbie. There is a good chance they will be found guilty because of who they are and not what they actually did, when we both know they are not guilty."

"Ok, Ok I hear you. I want you to go into court tomorrow, make an application to dismiss the charges in the interests of justice, but be certain to provide enough detail to make a clear record of why you are doing it."

I sat up most of the night writing out a speech to make before the judge the next day. When we arrived in court the next morning, before the jury was seated, I requested an opportunity to make an application to the court outside of the hearing of the jury members. The judge gave me an odd look, not knowing what I was up to, but he agreed to allow me to make my request.

I then spent close to half an hour outlining the various inconsistencies in the cabbie's story. I noted, among other things, that the cabbie had admitted on cross examination that the men had asked to be taken to the hospital. I also noted that the cabbie acknowledged that one of the men appeared to have a serious eye injury. This was hardly the circumstances in which someone would choose to conduct a robbery. I noted the lack of any weapon or other supporting evidence. After outlining all the other issues I had observed, I asked that the case be dismissed in the interests of justice.

When I finished the judge looked down at me sternly. I thought, now I am in trouble, but then he smiled and said: "thank you, if you had not done it, I would have."

The judge was clearly referring to the usual process in a jury trial. Generally, at the end of the prosecution's case the defense would move for a "directed verdict". While it rarely happened, the judge could rule there was insufficient evidence to present to the jury for consideration. Clearly here, the judge had already made up his mind for the same reasons I had asked to drop the case,

This story just goes to demonstrate some of the issues with prosecutors blindly moving forward because a grand jury issued an indictment. At the present time we hear of more and more instances of people convicted of crimes they did not commit, particularly when the accused are people of color and the victims are not.

We have seen an increasing number of cases where prosecutors, years after people were found guilty and incarcerated, have moved retroactively to dismiss charges.

The problem, at least back then, was the pressure to obtain convictions. I saw that at least a small number, and certainly not all, of my colleagues seemed to fear retribution for lack of successful prosecutions. Some of them appeared to fear that they might be demoted to less important positions in the office if they did not obtain convictions. Unfortunately, I suspect there is a similar pressure among some police officers to close cases and clear the case backlogs from their heavy workloads, even if all the evidence is not as solid as it should be before an arrest is made and charges filed. When presenting cases to a grand jury we were challenged to not only determine what to charge but to also decide if we really had a case that could be successfully prosecuted.

When those of us in the homicide bureau presented cases to the grand jury involving homicides, we also needed to decide whether to charge various degrees of murder and/or manslaughter. Much of this related to the office policies, at that time, stemming from the enormous caseload described earlier. With roughly four hundred homicides occurring annually in Brooklyn and the limited resources the office had to deal with the number of homicides, a rather strange set of policies were established in determining whether to charge homicides as murder or the lesser crime of manslaughter.

Although the process and policies changed over time, while I was in the Bureau, the eight riding assistants investigated the homicides and presented them to the grand jury. Thereafter, trials were conducted by other assistants assigned to the Supreme Court. The manslaughter cases were assigned to various assistants in those Supreme Court courtrooms covering various felony charges.

There were also two courtrooms in the courthouse devoted solely to trying cases where the grand jury had handed down murder indictments. In each of those two parts there was a senior trial assistant. They each had many years of experience trying murder cases and each had a completely different approach to conducting trials.

One assistant was loud and flamboyant and the other soft-spoken and matter of fact. I had a chance to watch them both and ultimately adopted the approach of the soft-spoken assistant, realizing that to be effective you had to be comfortable with the approach you used.

I must admit, watching the loud and flamboyant assistant was a bit more entertaining than watching the other. However, the job was not to entertain (although one of my trial supervisors did correctly suggest that it helped to put on a bit of show for the jury) but rather the job was to present your case and hopefully obtain a conviction.

Because there were only two courtrooms that handled murders and we were experiencing literally hundreds of homicides a year, the office had policies on whether to charge murder or manslaughter. The manslaughter charges could be tried in any courtroom in that Court and were not limited to being tried in the two overcrowded murder parts. There were some cases that clearly were not murder, like a death resulting from unintended consequences of such things as negligent actions. Such actions might be charged as criminally negligent homicide or perhaps involuntary manslaughter, depending upon the details of what had occurred.

However, there were other cases that were not as clear. Therefore, the office had guidelines which, like other guidelines sometimes seemed strange then and may seem even more bizarre today. One guideline was whether the death arose out of a case where a stranger assaulted and killed someone. Another factor in determining how to charge a homicide was whether the death occurred during a robbery. Yet another factor in determining the charge was if the death occurred between people who had certain close personal relationships.

Therefore, the general rule was that if there had been a close personal relationship between the victim and the accused, such as relative or boyfriend and girlfriend, then in many of those cases the charge would be reduced to manslaughter rather than a charge of murder. Yet, in the case where a stranger killed someone, and it was not due to an accident or negligence, the charge would be murder.

On one occasion I had a situation where the estranged husband of a woman tracked his wife to a store. As she exited the store he shot her four times, causing her death. Before presenting the case to the grand jury I discussed the case with my bureau chief, George, and confirmed, as it involved a husband and wife, even though they were separated, I would present to the grand jury the penal law provisions of the crime of manslaughter in the first degree, rather than murder. The procedures in the office required that I then go to the grand jury bureau, explain the case to the grand jury bureau chief and be assigned to present the case to one of the several grand juries sitting at any one time.

After reviewing the case with my chief, I went to the Grand Jury Bureau which was located in the Supreme Court courthouse. I stuck my head into the office of the chief of the grand jury bureau and was told to come in.

"What have you got today, Steve?"

"A guy who was in the middle of a nasty divorce from his wife, followed her to a store. He waited outside and when she came out, he fired gun into her, hitting her four times."

"What are you charging?"

"Manslaughter."

"Manslaughter! Are you kidding me? What could be more premeditated than a guy who tracks his wife down, waits for her and shoots her four times? Why are you not charging him with murder? This is not an accident or an unintended consequence of his actions. If there was ever an action by someone that met the definition of premeditated murder this would be it."

"You know the office policy. It is husband and wife. I checked with George. He confirmed I should charge manslaughter and not charge murder."

"That is nuts, I am calling George."

He then dialed my Bureau Chief. They had a rather heated discussion. In the end, consistent with office policy, we charged manslaughter, rather than murder.

In another instance, I handled a case of two roommates who got into an argument, and one stabbed the other to death during a struggle over a knife. When I presented the case and, as instructed because they were roommates and struggling over the knife when the stabbing occurred, I charged manslaughter.

After I had read the charge to the grand jury for their consideration, one of the grand jurors questioned why it was not murder. My somewhat strained explanation, made to fit the office policy, was that that they were struggling over the knife and there was no evidence that the intention was to cause the victim's death. While there actually was no such evidence that either intended to kill the other, the overriding basis for the decision was the office policy, as the two men were roommates. We did not charge people with such close personal relationships with murder under most circumstances.

15

CHAPTER 15
SELF-INFLICTED

In addition to having to go to the scenes of actual murders, we sometimes were called out to the scenes of situations that ultimately turned out to be some very sad suicides. Luckily, I never had to go to a scene where someone had jumped from the tenth floor of a high rise building to the ground below. I was told by those who had the misfortune of attending any of those or similar scenes that the body often exploded on impact with the ground. This resulted in something even more gruesome than the terrible things I already had to witness on the occasions I had to ride homicide.

As disgusting and gruesome as many of the scenes I attended turned out to be, a body on the ground that looked like a watermelon that had been dropped from a height, was more than I thought I could cope with. Luckily, I never had the opportunity to test my resilience in such circumstances. Yet, I did have several occasions when I was called out to the scene where someone had sadly taken their own life, for reasons fully known only to them.

Some of the ways people chose to end their lives were not only very sad but very strange. It seems that they often selected the most difficult and/or painful way to end their lives. However, perhaps for them this was a way of ending even greater pain than they were inflicting upon themselves as their last act. Therefore, these last acts were, apparently, at least for them, a relief. Although, their acts inflicted untold pain on those who cared for them.

One morning I was called to a scene where a man was found stabbed to death in his bathtub. I arrived at the scene shortly after the medical examiner had arrived. I was escorted through a rather dreary apartment at the top of a fifth-floor walkup. Lying in the dark, in an old clawfoot tub adjacent to the kitchen was a man covered in blood. As I entered, I introduced myself and asked what the situation we had was all about.

The medical examiner answer: "we have a suicide."

After looking at the body I questioned his conclusion.

"But how can that be? He has what looks like multiple stab wounds to his chest, with the knife still stuck in his chest. I don't understand how it can be that a person committing suicide could stab themselves multiple times in the chest?"

"Obviously the wound where the knife is stuck in his chest is what killed him. But these other two wounds merely broke the flesh and did not penetrate any further. They are what we call hesitation wounds. The poor man obviously tried a couple of times to stab himself, just breaking the flesh, before he finally realized that to accomplish his intended result, he had to just plunged the knife into his chest."

The police determined that there was no other evidence of anyone else being there or of any sort of struggle. He was discovered by a friend, who had a key to his apartment and went to check on him when he failed to answer his friend's telephone calls. In the following days, further investigation disclosed he had been suffering from depression and had made statements to more than one of his friends, over a period of months, about contemplating suicide. Those statements had increased in frequency in recent days just before his death. Although his friends had suggested that he seek help, he had not done so.

Therefore, the police closed the investigation on the basis of the information they obtained concerning his statements, the lack of any evidence that anyone else had been present. In addition to that information his fingerprints were on the knife in his chest, and we had the medical examiner's conclusion upon examining the body that this was a suicide.

On another occasion I was called to a single-family home in an upper middle-class neighborhood, as a body had been found inside the house. When I arrived, I observed a well-kept lawn in front of a tidy single family cape style home. There were a few people, apparently from the neighborhood standing in front of the property on the sidewalk milling around. I went up to the police officer in front of the house and identified myself. He directed me to go around to the back door of the house and said I would find the officers just inside.

I entered the house through a small eat in kitchen that connected to the adjacent dining room. As I entered the doorway that connected to the dining room, I saw three young police officers sitting at a large dining room table. They each had a paper coffee cup in front of them and were chatting about baseball, without an apparent care in the world. Obviously, they were waiting for the medical examiner to arrive to check the body, so that it could be released.

As I entered the dining room I again identified myself to the police officers at the table.

"Where is the body?"

One of the cops pointed to a sheet draped over a doorknob at the end of the room. It seemed a bit odd, to say the least. but I walked over and lifted the sheet. There was a gray haired, elderly woman hanging by her neck from a rope attached to the doorknob. Her legs were bent, and it appeared that none of her weight was resting on the floor. Her face was literally blue, and it was clear, at least to me, she had strangled on the rope. I put the sheet back over her head and waited for the medical examiner to arrive.

A few minutes later the medical examiner came in through the back door, he confirmed we had a suicide. The woman lived alone and was found by a relative when she did not respond to telephone calls.

There were no other signs of a struggle or anything being out of place. As a result, there was nothing further for me to investigate.

Thinking of her choking on the rope around her neck while all she had to do was put her foot on the floor caused me to wonder just how desperate someone must be to strangle themselves hanging from a doorknob.

In another instance, a fellow hung himself from the handrail of a staircase in a manner similar to the poor lady who hung herself from the doorknob.

There were other strange incidents I heard about but did not actually see.

Another example was a desperate person, hanging himself from the steering wheel of his car with a rope through the window. Of course, perhaps the strangest of all was the fellow who came into the hospital complaining of a terrible headache. The headache was no doubt caused by the screwdriver he had hammered into and was sticking out of his forehead. He did survive, at least that incident.

16

CHAPTER 16
INVESTIGATING THE POLICE

The full title of our bureau was Homicide and Investigations. At that time, because of some recent police scandals, there was a special prosecutor's office created by the City of New York that had been appointed to investigate police corruption. Irrespective of the special prosecutors' investigations, in addition to homicides, we occasionally were called upon to also investigate claims of wrongdoing by members of the police department.

Anything that was particularly serious or appeared to be part of any wide scale police corruption was either picked up directly by the special prosecutor's office or referred to the special prosecutor by the individual county district attorneys' offices. However, cases that appeared to be isolated and relatively minor incidents, involving potentially improper conduct by the police, fell within the jurisdiction of the district attorney of each county.

In Brooklyn, those matters were referred to the Homicide and Investigations Bureau and landed on the desks of the riding assistants. Most of the time the complaints turned out to be nothing of any significant consequence. Occasionally, like our regular homicide investigations, we turned up something so bizarre that when other members of the bureau heard about it their initial reaction was that it had to be a made-up story.

One night I was out on my usual homicide calls when I was beeped by the office. I called the office from the precinct where I was conducting interviews, expecting to be told about yet another homicide

I had to deal with. Instead, I was advised that a man had been struck and killed by a car on Ocean Parkway, which is a main street running north and south through a large section of Brooklyn. There was nothing suspicious about the incident. It was clearly an accident, and the driver remained at the scene until the police arrived.

I immediately asked why I was being called about it if there was nothing suspicious about the death. It turned out the issue that came up which required the attention of the DA's office was the fact that while the man was lying on the street, one of the officers on the scene had noticed some dollar bills sticking out of the man's pants pocket. The man was pronounced dead at the scene of the accident and transported, by ambulance, to the morgue. However, when the man's body arrived at the morgue and his belongings were inventoried, there was no money found in any of his pockets.

As a result, it was suspected that at some point, either at the scene of the accident or while he was being transported to the morgue, someone had gone through his pockets and stolen the money that had been observed at the scene of the accident by the first member of the police department to arrive.

This seemed like a minor matter. But, since there were police officers involved in guarding the body before it was transported to the morgue, there was the possibility that a police officer had taken the money. Our instructions from George were that whenever there was a case of potential criminal activity by the police, we must call him out, no matter when it happened and no matter how late at night it might be.

As a general rule, as these were potentially high-profile issues, George wanted to attend interviews of all of the parties involved in any potential police misdeeds. This was most unpleasant for the riding assistant involved in the investigation, as I had the misfortune to experience on one occasion.

George hovered in the corner of the room where the interviews were being conducted by the riding assistant. George watched your every move, to be certain you were "properly" conducting the interviews. Just to be as imposing as possible, aside from being a large man, he did not take off his coat. Further, trying to look like the detective, played by Gene Hackman in the movie the French Connection, which was popular at the time, he stood there with what was referred to as a "pork pie" hat propped on his head.

He said nothing. Yet, his constant stares, and occasional grunts and grimaces, during the process were most distracting. The assistant conducting the interviews would try to focus on the task of interviewing the parties involved in the incident. At the same time the assistant would be trying not to do or say anything that would set George off and result in a tongue lashing the next day or even out on the street when the interviews were completed.

It was now nearly midnight. I thought, especially as I had nothing else pending and could otherwise go home, this was a minor issue that could be dealt with at a later date. I thought I could direct everyone to appear in the office in two days, as it was my regular day off, on the day following my day of riding homicide. As per previous instructions, I called the boss at home. Of course, making the call to him at home, when it was close to midnight, as expected, woke him up, only adding to his usual grumpy disposition.

"George, sorry to call so late, this is Steve. I am riding tonight and just received a call that we have a case where a man was struck and killed by a car. Someone noticed dollar bills sticking out of his pocket at the scene of the accident but when the body arrived at the morgue, there was no money found in his pockets. Apparently, between the police on the scene, ambulance crew and morgue attendants there are several people who will have to be interviewed.

I called you because of your instructions that we let you know anytime there is any possible police corruption involved in an incident. However, this seems like a relatively minor situation. I think, in view of the late hour and the number of people involved, I should just arrange for all involved to come to the office the day after tomorrow when I am back in the office. In the interim the police can also do a more detailed investigation into what happened. Perhaps they can come up with enough information to even avoid the necessity of continuing our investigation or at least narrow down the number of people we have to interview."

From his tone of voice, I could tell he was annoyed at being awakened concerning this trivial matter. However, also aware that I was following his very specific instructions to contact him, no matter what time of day or night, regarding any possible police corruption issues he therefore responded:

"Steve, a good investigator follows up as soon as possible while the evidence and memories are fresh. Delay can cause people to forget key bits of information that may not immediately appear significant. You should go there tonight and interview everyone involved. Be certain to write up your report and I will review it when I get into the office tomorrow morning."

"Alright. I assume that means you will not be coming out to the precinct while I conduct the interviews?"

"No, you can handle it yourself. Just be certain to get me a full report, on my desk before I get in tomorrow morning at 9."

Clearly, I was being taught a lesson for waking him up at midnight. Also, just to make my life even more miserable, he had given me specific instructions to be certain the report was on his desk before 9 a.m. Therefore, no matter when I finished the interviews in this case, and no matter when I finished up with anything else that came in after those interviews, I had to get someone to drive me to the office to drop off my handwritten report. Only after the report was delivered could I go home. Now I was stuck. I also had to cover any possible angle, or he would be all over me for not conducting what he considered to be a proper and thorough investigation.

I called the detective in charge of the incident and told him I would be coming in to interview all parties who were involved in any manner with the situation. I told him I wanted every one of the parties involved in the incident waiting for me when I arrived, so that I could take statements from all of them.

I already had a court reporter with me. I went to the desk Sargent in the precinct I was calling from and arranged transportation to the precinct where they would all hopefully be gathered, awaiting my arrival.

When I arrived and was taken to the interview room, it was full. Waiting for me were the police officers who first arrived at the scene of the accident. Also, there were the police officers who arrived at the scene later to help direct traffic and deal with any onlookers while the body was being removed. Attorneys from the police union (the PBA) were also there to protect the rights of all the officers involved in the incident. We also had the ambulance attendants who transported the body to the morgue, the different morgue attendants who first unloaded the body from the ambulance, the morgue attendant who moved the body into the morgue and the morgue attendant who inventoried the dead man's possessions in the morgue. It looked like it would be quite a party, starting after midnight.

It seemed that the most logical course of inquiry was to start from the beginning. In that way I could go step by step tracing the movement of the body, his clothes, and belongings, through each person, in chronological order. I would have to determine who observed or touched the body while it was in the street, being transported to the morgue, being removed from the ambulance and lying in the morgue. I could also determine who had seen the money and at what point it appeared to have gone missing.

By the time we had the stenographer set up and I had figured out who should be in the room with each witness, as well as the order of the interviews, it was about 1 a.m. I would have to interview about eleven people before I finished. But with the threat of George's review hanging over me I had to be as thorough as possible.

I asked all the witnesses to be placed in another room and instructed them not to discuss the matter with each other. Then I began to take each witness separately, while the others were kept out of the room where the interviews were taking place, so that we could get each person's independent version of what happened.

We took the witnesses in the order in which they interacted with the dead man's body. Of course, each police officer was accompanied by his PBA attorney to ensure I did nothing to violate the police officer's rights.

We started with the first officer on the scene and his PBA lawyer. In that interview we established that when the officer arrived the man was sprawled on the road and obviously dead. There appeared to be the corners of one or more-dollar bills sticking out of the top of his front right pants pocket. Likewise, the two officers who arrived next described the location and condition of the body and confirmed that they had also noticed the dollar bills protruding from the pocket of his pants.

The EMTs who arrived at the scene shortly after the police, confirmed the man was dead. They acknowledged they had also seen the corners of the dollar bills sticking out of the dead man's pocket. The ambulance attendants, who loaded the body onto the ambulance, to be transported to the morgue also noticed the corners of the dollar bills protruding from the pocket.

With each witness, I asked if anyone touched or moved the money, or saw anyone touch or move the money, and they all denied doing anything or seeing anyone doing anything with the money.

The morgue attendants who unloaded the body did not recall seeing any dollar bills, which made me slightly suspicious of the ambulance attendants. Yet, the ambulance attendants had not denied seeing the dollar bills which would have been a reasonable way to cover up, if they had taken them. However, I needed to complete all the interviews before I could reach any conclusions.

Finally, after about two hours of interviewing the witnesses in the order in which they interacted with the dead man, I interviewed the morgue attendant who had gone through the dead man's belongings.

He was the one who had inventoried the belongings and made no notation of there being any money in the dead man's possession.

"Sir, when you went through the belongings of the deceased, did you find any dollar bills?"

"No, but I did find some one dollar coupons?"

"Can you explain what they looked like?"

"Yes, they looked like dollar bills. They were green and had a one in the corner, similar to what would be on a one dollar bill."

"Where would they be now?"

"They are at the morgue. We inventory all the belongings of anybody brought to the morgue and do not throw out anything that we find on the body."

"Then can I assume if you went back to the morgue with an officer, you could retrieve the coupons you just described to me and bring them here."

"Sure, I can do that. I know where they are."

I looked at the detective in charge and asked if he could have an officer drive the gentleman to the morgue and come back with the morgue attendant and the coupons he had described. The detective immediately made arrangements for the attendant to be taken back to the morgue to recover the coupons. Then all the police officers, PBA attorneys and attendants sat in the office and waited for the morgue attendant to return with the evidence.

It took about forty minutes for them to go to the morgue and return. I had no cell phone or ipad in those days, so the only thing I could do was just sit there and wait. At that point we had been at this "investigation" for nearly three hours.

The police officer finally arrived with the morgue attendant and the coupons. It was now four in the morning. I had tied up half a dozen police officers, their PBA attorneys, EMTs and morgue attendants to conduct a thorough investigation of this potential crime involving what turned out to be dollar off coupons.

There were three coupons. Sure enough, they were green and made to look like one-dollar bills. I showed them to the officers from the scene of the accident and they acknowledged the coupons were likely what they had observed. I took a polaroid photo of them and closed my investigation.

I made certain to file a full report, with all the details concerning who was interviewed and what they said, with the boss so that there would be no question that I had followed his instructions to conduct a full and thorough investigation of all possible aspects of the incident.

I have no idea how much this "investigation" cost the City of New York in overtime for the police. EMTs and morgue attendants who sat around for over three hours while we conducted this inquiry which George determined could not wait for two days. But surely justice was done that night.

I knew George wanted the report of this incident waiting for him when he got into the office the next morning. I was exhausted at this point and decided if there were no other calls that night I could get a few hours sleep. Since my wife had to get up early anyway, I would go home, set my alarm, get up early and drop the report off with the officer on duty at the office before George got in at nine in the morning.

The next morning, I dragged myself out of bed, got dressed and even though it was technically my day off, I ran into the office and dropped off the report for George's review before he got in.

On the following day I was still dragging a bit. As a result, I did not get into the office until nine fifteen. As I entered the building and walked toward the elevators, I saw the unmistakable back of George waiting at the elevator. Just as I got up to the elevators, the door to one opened, George walked into the elevator, and I walked in behind him. As the door closed, he turned around and saw me.

George lifted his hand and looked down at his wristwatch and scowled. He looked up at me and said:

"Mr. Silverberg, we start work at nine not nine fifteen every morning."

I don't know what got into me. Maybe it was the fact that I was still tired from being out nearly all night two nights before. Maybe it was the fact that I had to drive into the office early in the morning on my day off, the day before, to drop off the report he probably never read. Or maybe it was just my basic wise guy personality.

I looked at George and smiled and said:

"You are right, you should really try to get in on time."

As the words came out of my mouth, I held my breath expecting an explosion. Instead, there was a barely discernible grunt and nothing else.

17

CHAPTER 17
CHRISTMAS EVE

When the time came for someone to cover Christmas Day and Christmas Eve, the rotation was changed. Therefore, two Jewish members of the Bureau were selected to cover the holiday period. This relieved those observing the Christmas Holiday from having to spend the holiday visiting dead bodies instead of enjoying some time with their families. I was selected for the Christmas Eve shift at riding homicide, which turned out to be one of the more unusual and, in retrospect, one of the strangest and even amusing experiences of my life.

Early in the day, I was called out to interview witnesses in a shooting. I arrived at the 13th Homicide Bureau, which covered several of the precincts that tended to have many homicides on a regular basis, throughout the year. I was well known to the detectives; due to the large number of homicides I had covered there, on a nearly weekly basis, over several months.

As I entered the detective bureau offices of the 13th Homicide Bureau, the two detectives, who knew me as Silverberg looked up and greeted me as I walked into the office. I soon learned that the people sitting on a bench on the side of the room were the witnesses I was there to interview.

Yet, that did not impede the detectives' holiday spirit. After all, it was Christmas Eve and the detectives were apparently in an unusually jovial holiday mood. The two detectives, upon noticing me walking into the room, stood up in front of those same witnesses, who were waiting nervously, as they were told they had to be interviewed by the assistant district attorney (me). The detectives then locked arms and began to sing at the top of their lungs to the tune of the Christmas Carol Silver Bells:

"Silverballs, silverballs, its Christmas time in the city,...".

With that introduction I had to try to act seriously and take the witnesses, who had just sat through the entertainment, to an interview room for questioning about a homicide they had seen earlier that day. Yet, in a day and night that would test my stamina, and in some respects my sanity, I had just experienced the most normal part of a very, very long and strange day and night.

After taking the somewhat routine statements of the witnesses, I went back to the office. The rest of the normal workday was generally quiet, with the exception of an occasional call from a police officer with a legal question, which as the designated riding assistant for that day, I was tasked to answer. I also worked on my old open cases.

Shortly before 5 p.m. I received a call that the owner of a liquor store had been shot during a holdup. He had been rushed to the hospital but died on his way to the hospital. I was told there would be witnesses at the local precinct. I arranged to be brought to the 61st precinct, which was located, in those days, in a quiet neighborhood on Avenue U a bit north of the Sheepshead Bay Area.

Upon arrival, I was told the detective was on a stakeout, as they believed they knew who did the shooting and where he lived. I was told the detective felt the capture was imminent. Of course, trying to capture the shooter was critical to resolving the case. I was also told the detective expected to return to the precinct shortly with the suspect in custody. Therefore, it was suggested that I should wait for him. There was no one else present who knew much about the case and no sign of any witnesses.

I had no other calls backed up yet. I didn't want to leave, only to be called back, in an hour, or less. Therefore, I waited around, hopeful that I might have a suspect to question. After waiting just about an hour, with nothing to do but stare at the bare walls of a room that needed a fresh coat of paint, the detective showed up. But he did not have a suspect with him. It was also clear from the strong odor of alcohol on the detective's breath that his stakeout had been conducted rather thoroughly at a bar.

After all, some celebration was needed when you were a police detective working on a murder investigation on Christmas Eve. Of course, it was also possible the suspect lived at the bar. The detective advised that they had some potential leads on the shooter, but it would be some time before they had anything for me. He said he would contact me when he had someone for me to interview. At that moment, there was absolutely nothing for me to do there.

In the interim, not long before the detective arrived, I had gotten beeped again and was told there had been an attempted holdup at gunpoint of a bodega owner and that the owner had shot the holdup man with a gun licensed to the bodega owner. It appeared there was no criminal act by the owner. He was in the hospital with a gunshot wound as he had acted in self-defense using a licensed gun.

However, the robber had died at the hospital. There were several witnesses to the incident. I needed to interview the witnesses, to establish no cause for an arrest of the store owner so the matter could be closed.

The new case was on the other side of Brooklyn. Tony was off for Christmas Eve. As a result, I needed to have a police officer drive me to the other precinct to conduct the interviews of the witnesses to the attempted holdup of the bodega and the shooting of the holdup man.

I went down to the Desk Sargent and explained that I needed a patrol car to take me to the 90th precinct in the Williamsburg section of Brooklyn. As usual, I was known by the Desk Sargent, even though this was one of the less active precincts for our homicide investigations. Continuing with the insanity that was to be the hallmark of this shift riding homicide, the Desk Sargent said:

"As I recall you live near here, don't you?"

"Yes, why?"

"It being Christmas Eve, we are short-handed. We need patrolmen to cover the calls we are getting, as well as conducting normal street patrols. I could give you an RMP (police talk for a patrol car) to take for your use tonight and you can just bring it back in the morning, whenever you are ready."

Immediately, my mind raced through the scenario. I am driving a patrol car in civilian clothes and get stopped by the police. How do I explain why I have a patrol car? There had been numerous instances lately of people shooting at police cars, how do I protect myself? What if I have an accident? There was no parking lot where I lived. The on-street parking was generally difficult to find, particularly during a holiday when people had family visit. When I went back to my apartment house later, where would I park the patrol car? Also, when I brought the patrol car back the next morning, how would I explain to the next Desk Sargent on duty at the desk in the morning why I had been driving around in a patrol car all night?

While the idea of having my own patrol car with lights and a siren had a certain appeal, it all seemed like an insane idea with the potential for multiple problems. As tempting as it might be to drive around Brooklyn in my own patrol car on Christmas Eve, I decided to decline the kind offer.

"No, I don't think that is a very good idea. I don't want the responsibility of driving an RMP that I have no right to be driving. Please arrange for someone to drive me."

A short time later I was taken by an officer in a patrol car. As we were literally located on the other side of the County from where we were heading, between traffic from last minute shoppers, people going to family dinners and the distance we had to cover, it took about forty-five minutes to get there from the 61st precinct, located not terribly far from Sheepshead Bay, to the 90th precinct in the Williamsburg section of Brooklyn.

Upon arriving at the other precinct, I thanked the officer who drove me and went inside the somewhat shabby older building. As I approached the detective's office there were three witnesses sitting on a bench outside the office. As I walked by the witnesses with my trench coat, hat and briefcase, I heard one witness turn to the others and say, "that must be the DA." As I was all of twenty-six years old, I was pleased that my outfit gave the appearance I had been hoping for, when I chose it for whatever effect it might have.

I entered the detective's office. I identified myself to the somewhat younger than usual detective, who I had not previously met. The unlucky stenographer, who had the night shift, was already there and set up. The detective filled me in on what they had found out about the incident. It sounded like a relatively straight forward situation that I merely had to document.

As I had been advised in the call I had received, the detective confirmed a guy with a gun walked into the bodega and demanded money. The owner, who had a licensed gun pulled it from a drawer under the cash register. He exchanged gunfire with the robber. The owner was wounded and was currently receiving treatment at the hospital. He was expected to recover. The robber had received a fatal wound and died on the way to the hospital.

My job was to make a record of what had happened, to confirm the owner had acted in self-defense and there was no basis for charging the owner with any crime. I confirmed with the detectives they had the two guns in their possession and the gun the store owner had used was licensed. I told him to bring in the first of the three witnesses so I could take all the statements.

The detective escorted a heavyset woman who, appeared to be in her early fifties and must have weighed over two hundred and fifty pounds into the room. As she entered the small room containing a desk and a few folding chairs, she was directed to take a seat opposite me. She was obviously very nervous as she took her seat. Her hands were shaking. Her head turned from side to side as her eyes were darting around the room looking at everyone with a distressed expression on her face. She didn't seem to know where to look first. Clearly, already distressed at having witnessed the gun fight in the bodega, the unfamiliar scene playing out in front of her only added to her distress.

The detective in charge of the investigation sat very close behind her. It probably did not help her nerves having him sitting there practically breathing down her neck in those cramped quarters. In addition, while she knew he was there, she was also unable to see him sitting there behind her. There was the court stenographer with the strange looking machine that most people had not yet seen on television at that time and this guy in a suit (me) sitting in front of her.

"Hello, I am Assistant District Attorney Silverberg."

She began to shake even more.

"I am here to ask you about an incident I am told you witnessed earlier this evening."

Before I could ask her my first question her eyes rolled back in her head, she fainted, and she slid off her chair onto the floor. The detective and his partner, who had entered the room shortly before she came in. jumped up and tried to arouse her, but she was out cold. They checked her pulse, and she was alive but unconscious. After several further attempts to bring her out of her unconscious state, the detective opened the door to the interview room and called for assistance by other police officers.

In the less than five minutes the poor woman was in the interview room, four police officers carried her out in front of and directly passed the other two witnesses who were sitting on the bench outside the door waiting to go in next. One can only imagine what went through the other witness's minds as they watched the woman being carried out unconscious by four police officers from the room where she was supposedly just asked a few questions about the shooting they had witnessed.

Unfortunately, I had to proceed with the other two witnesses who had seen the woman being carried out. Next, they brought in a young woman. Understandably, she was shaking. She had just seen the last witness being carried out of the room unconscious by four police officers. I wondered what she was thinking we had done to the poor woman and what her own fate might be if perhaps we did not like her responses to our questions.

She took the seat opposite me and the detective again sat behind her, as he had done with the previous witness. I tried to reassure the young woman, as best I could, everything was alright and there was nothing to be concerned about. Then I began the formal interview.

"Hello, I am Assistant District Attorney Silverberg. I am here to ask about an incident I am told you witnessed earlier today."

With that the detective, who was sitting behind the witness, rolled his eyes into the back of his head. Stuck his tongue out of the corner of his mouth and pretended to slump in the seat behind the witness. I tried to keep my composure as with each question he repeated his little pantomime.

Aside from the fact that he was being completely unprofessional, we were dealing with a serious incident in which someone was killed and he was acting like a high school student making fun of a teacher. I was tempted to yell at him, but I did not want to do anything else to make the poor, frightened witness more nervous. I tried my best to ignore the detective and not let his repeated antics cause me to start laughing in the middle of the interview with this poor, terrified young woman. In retrospect this was just the lead into what was to come next that evening.

The witness basically told the same story the detective had relayed to me. I was able to finish questioning the witnesses, including the woman who had fainted. She had recovered shortly after she was carried out and felt well enough to speak with me. They all told the same story, that the robber had pulled the gun and there was an exchange of gunfire.

It was clear that the witnesses had a frightening experience, which explained their demeanor when I spoke with them. It was also clear we had no evidence that the bodega owner had done anything other than act in self-defense against an armed robber who was ready, willing and able to shoot him.

As I was standing and speaking with the detective, who clearly totally lacked professionalism, he picked up the gun that had been used in the shooting and pointed it at me. I looked at him in disbelief and in an angry tone said:

"What the hell are you doing?"

"No, need to worry, it's not loaded."

"I don't care if it is not loaded don't point it at me and put it down. Why would you play with the gun?"

Consistent with his otherwise childish behavior during the whole process, he made a face and put the gun down.

I had been beeped again while I was finishing my interview of the witnesses. When I called in, I was advised they were now finally ready for me at the 61st precinct.

I then went to the Desk Sargent of the precinct with the stenographer. I explained to the Desk Sargent that we needed transport back to the 61st precinct, The Desk Sargent told us to go out to the parking lot and a patrolman would meet us there to take us to the precinct.

Outside, in the parking lot we were met by a young patrolman who looked to be about my age. He took us to a patrol car. I got in the front passenger side seat and the stenographer jumped in the back with his machine. The patrolman got in turned to me and said:

"We are going to the six-one?"

"Yes"

"My wife is having Christmas dinner with her family a few blocks from there. My boss thinks it is going to take about an hour and a half for me to drive you there and come back. If I can make up some time, I could stop in at my in laws apartment for a little Christmas dinner with the family. Would it be alright with you, if I put on a little speed so I could reduce the time getting you to the six-one."

Having no concept of what he meant exactly by putting "on a little speed" I responded:

"Of course, how could I say no on Christmas Eve to a request to have dinner with your wife."

I fully expected he might take some shortcuts or just travel a little above the speed limit so he could get fifteen minutes with the family, before heading back to work. He pulled out of the parking lot and proceeded at a normal speed. However, as soon as we were about a block away from the police station, he put on the emergency lights and siren and took off at a very high rate of speed, as if he were responding to an emergency. I could not see the speedometer, but we were clearly driving as if we were driving, above the speed limit, on an Interstate.

The ride was something akin to an amusement park roller coaster, only more frightening because there were cars, bicycles, and pedestrians in the way. We alternated between going down the wrong side of the road to, at one point, driving on the sidewalk to get around some traffic.

There are two things that stick out most in my memory, about this terror ride. The first was the portion of the drive down a sidewalk. As we proceeded to drive on the sidewalk, only a little bit slower than we had been going on the road, there was an entrance stairway to a building jutting out over the sidewalk. The stairway was directly opposite a telephone pole. I am convinced, to this day, as we passed between the stairway and the pole, the space was so narrow that if the car had an extra coat of paint, we would not have made it through without hitting the pole or the stairway. Yet, he hardly slowed down as we passed between them while driving on the sidewalk at a speed that also likely exceeded the speed limit.

The other memory is of a woman pushing a baby carriage crossing the street as we sped down the wrong side of the road. The patrol car swerved into the other lane to avoid hitting either her or the carriage she was pushing in front of her. Luckily with the emergency light flashing and the siren screeching other cars made way for us so that we could get to the "emergency" Christmas dinner in a timely manner.

I was not wearing a seatbelt, and I braced my knees against the dashboard in case we had to abruptly stop. At one point the young patrolman turned to me with a bit of a grin on his face, as if to make fun of me and asked: "am I making you nervous?" I did not want to seem like I was just some weak young civilian, too soft to deal with the excitement. I smiled at him and lied "no, not nervous at all, do whatever you need to do."

As we pulled up in front of the 61st precinct, I looked at my watch and realized, while it had taken us forty-five-minutes to drive to the other precinct, our return trip had taken the grand total of seven minutes. Amazingly, we were also unscathed, except for my heart pounding. I turned to the young patrolman:

"I guess you can have that Christmas dinner with your family."

"Yes, thank you."

"Merry Christmas officer."

As I got out of the patrol car, I looked in the back seat and could not see the stenographer. I knew he had been there when we started our little adventure. I wondered where he could be, as I was certain if he had fallen out of the patrol car we would have noticed. I opened the back door of the patrol car.

Instead of being on the back seat, he was lying on his stomach on the floor of the back seat. Slowly, he crawled out of the car on his hands and knees and onto the sidewalk. While he was prone on the sidewalk he leaned down and kissed the ground. While I laughed at him, I totally understood and sympathized with his actions. He stood up, reached into the car to get his stenographic machine, and closed the door. The car made a "u" turn and took off for Christmas dinner.

We went into the precinct to take statements, but nothing else that night was memorable. My wild ride, with a young cop whose boss thought he was taking an hour and a half, instead of a fourteen-minute, round trip to another precinct, left the rest of the night as a blur.

18

CHAPTER 18
EXTORTION

As part of our investigation duties, besides homicides, we would be asked to look into crimes that had come to our attention by individuals coming into the office to make a complaint or, in some cases, through our informants.

One day when I was on rotation a man, we'll call Stanley, came to the office claiming he was the victim of extortion. He claimed that someone he knew was trying to get him to pay over a large sum of money with a threat of violence against him, if he did not turn over the money that was being demanded. The man appeared a bit odd. From the way he explained what was happening I thought he might be imagining the entire situation.

He had no physical evidence of the claimed extortion and based upon his odd demeanor I was not certain whether what he described was really occurring or was a result of his imagination. In addition, without any evidence of the events taking place there was nothing we could do. If we had the police approach the person Stanley claimed was trying to extort money from him, the man could just deny it and potentially place Stanley in physical danger, if the threats were real.

I asked Stanley if he had a tape recorder. He said he did. I suggested that the next time he received one of the telephone calls from the man threatening him that he record the call by purchasing a simple device that could connect the recorder to the telephone. I gave him my card so he could reach me if anything developed. We shook hands and he left. I breathed a sigh of relief assuming I would never hear from him again.

A week later he called me and said he had gotten another telephone call. He had purchased the device I suggested and had made a tape recording of the conversation. I had him come to the office with the tape.

Much to my surprise, the conversation he recorded clearly indicated the man on the other end of the call was demanding that Stanley withdraw two thousand dollars from his bank account. The money was to be delivered to the man in two days. He indicated he would be waiting for Stanley across the street from Stanley's bank at a specified time. I called in one of our detectives and we arranged to have Stanley set up with a wire transmitter and for members of the local police precinct to be present to arrest the extortionist when the money was hand delivered to him.

Two days later everything was set to proceed and immediately after the event I was provided with a recording of what transpired, The tape allowed me to listen to the process of wiring Stanley and him delivering the money. Stanley was clearly nervous. We listened to his nearly constant chatter during the process of setting up the wire and the events that followed.

After Stanley was fitted with the wire recording device he announced he had to use the bathroom. We had the full effect of him going to the men's room, closing the door and the sound of him urinating in the urinal. After that he walked several blocks to the bank, narrating nervously all along the way.

He entered the bank and requested a withdrawal from his savings account of two thousand dollars in one-hundred-dollar bills. He put the money in a paper bag and exited the bank. He had gotten a description of the late model red Ford convertible to look for across the street once he had the money. Obviously, he had given that information to the police and they had stationed men in civilian clothing nearby to move in once the money was delivered.

We listened to Stanley's narration and the subsequent dialog.

"Ok, I am crossing the street now and see the red Ford in the middle of the block."

A few seconds later:

"Stanley, do you have the money I told you to get."

"Yes, right here in the paper bag."

"Hand it over."

We heard the paper bag rustling.

"Don't worry it is all there."

"Just checking Stanley before I let you go"

Just then we heard several people running and:

"Hold it right there, police, put your hands where we can see them."

The guy extorting Stanley was arrested. We had his threats and the transaction on tape and the police caught him next to Stanley holding the bag of money. He was subsequently convicted of multiple charges.

19

CHAPTER 19
MY FINAL HOMICIDE

There I was in the early morning hours, standing in the misty glow of a streetlamp. The police officer who was depositing his dinner in the street had finally stopped vomiting. Then the detective in charge at the scene came out of the same row house, the young police officer had so rapidly exited a few minutes earlier.

As the detective approached the stenographer, Frank, again said:

"I am not going in there."

"I will find somewhere that is far enough from the body that you will not see it. Stay out here until I call for you."

The detective a man about five foot seven inches, with dark curly hair, looked like he was in his mid-forties. I had not worked with him before. Then we introduced ourselves and I followed him into the row house.

He took me into the living room. There I saw the most disgusting scene I had ever experienced in all the awful homicide scenes I had visited in eight months. Sprawled on the floor was what I was told was a woman. The entire bottom half of her face was missing. One eye was hanging out of the eye socket and the other eye was on the floor next to her. The rest of the floor surrounding her was scattered with blood and other pieces of her head and face.

"What happened."

"According to her son, who is thirteen years old, his parents were having a terrible argument. The son left the room because he couldn't stand what was going on. A couple of minutes later he heard a loud bang and came down here. His mother was lying on the floor like that and his father was holding a shotgun to his own head, Before the kid could say or do anything the father pulled the trigger."

"What happened to the father?"

"The kid called the police and when the ambulance arrived they transported the father who was still alive to the hospital. I am awaiting an update on him, but it does not sound likely he will survive.

"I hate to do this. It would be good to get a statement from the kid. If the father dies that will give us enough to close this out and not have to bother the poor kid again. Is he still around?"

"Two doors down, a neighbor brought him over to their house."

"Can you ask if we can go over there and speak with the kid for a couple of minutes? I will make it as short as possible. Also, what is his name?"

"He is Freddy. Yes, I will go ask the neighbor if there is somewhere we can sit for a few minutes and ask Freddy a few questions."

I went outside to wait and spoke to Frank. I explained he would not have to go in the house but that we were arranging to go to the house of a neighbor where the victim's son, who was a witness to the homicide, was staying.

The detective came out and escorted us to the neighbor's house. As we entered the front door, we were greeted by a brown-haired woman, whose eyes were red, apparently from crying, who looked to be in her thirties and looked very sad.

"I know you have to speak to Freddy. But, as you can imagine, he has been through a terrible time. Please do it as quickly as possible."

I responded:

"I completely understand what a horrible experience this has been for him. I will try to be as brief and as gentle as possible. I will only cover what I absolutely must cover and then leave him alone."

"Thank you."

She escorted us to the kitchen where Freddy was sitting at a 1950's style dinette set looking down at the floor with his hands in his lap.

We walked in and I introduced myself.

"Freddy, I am Mr. Silverberg from the District Attorney's Office. First, I am so sorry for your terrible loss."

He began to sob a little.

"I need to ask you a few questions and this gentleman is going to type up your answers so that hopefully we will not have to bother you again. Are you OK to answer a few questions?"

He nodded silently.

Frank set up his machine. I did my usual formal introduction and asked Freddy what he had seen. He described the situation exactly as the detective had described it to me. We were out of there in less than five minutes.

I got a patrol car to drive me home. It was now nearly three in the morning. I could not sleep. Despite all the terrible things I had seen before as an assistant DA riding homicide, I had never seen anything that awful. And the thought of poor Freddy having witnessed the event made it all the more terrible. I paced the living room the rest of the night. My wife got up to go to work and came looking for me.

"What is going on, you still have your suit on, did you just get home?"

"No, I have been home for several hours."

"Then why haven't you come to bed?"

"I saw something terrible last night that I can't get out of my head and can't sleep."

"A murder?"

"Yes, a terrible, bloody mess, I really don't want to discuss it."

"OK, I will leave you alone, I have to get to work anyway."

My wife got ready and left for work.

I was supposed to have brought in my report from the night before but did not feel like going to the office, Also, it was my last week in homicide, there was not much George could do to punish me.

I changed out of my suit, got cleaned up, had a little breakfast and took the subway to Manhattan. I spent the day aimlessly wandering around Manhattan trying to get the scene from my last night riding homicide out of my head.

THE END

Acknowledgements

First, I would like to thank my many friends who, over the years, encouraged me to write this book. I hope they will not be disappointed when they see the finished product. I would also like to thank my friends Marc Weiner, Phil Gerstein and Fred Devan for their thoughtful comments on an earlier draft of the book. Special thanks to Aaron Silverberg for his detailed review of the next to last draft and to Arlene Silverberg for her thoughts and assistance in formatting the book cover.

About the Author

Steven M. Silverberg has practiced law for over fifty years, starting as a prosecutor in the Brooklyn District Attorney's Office, part of which is the subject of this book, and then as a Town Prosecutor for the largest Town in Westchester New York. After about seven years as a prosecutor he went into private law practice, ultimately co-founding the law firm of Silverberg Zalantis LLC which focuses on zoning, land use, municipal and environmental law. Over the years he co-authored a book and authored a number of articles on various legal subjects related to land use and environmental law.

www.ingramcontent.com/pod-product-compliance
Lightning Source LLC
Chambersburg PA
CBHW070630030426
42337CB00020B/3974